With biblical wisdom and dec[...] and Sally Clarkson offer families a treasure in [...] It's a humble yet urgent message to each of us pursuing this messy mission of raising kids to love Jesus and love the world. *We* are the lifegivers. It's not a formula, program, or set of methods. It's a way of life. With God's help, we will pass on what we possess, giving the life of God to our children. No matter what stage of parenting you are in, you will find *The Lifegiving Parent* challenging, helpful, and encouraging.

> PATRICK AND RUTH SCHWENK, founders of TheBetterMom.com and ForTheFamily.org and authors of *For Better or for Kids: A Vow to Love Your Spouse with Kids in the House*

With a beautiful balance of biblical teaching, practicality, and an understanding of the challenges parenting brings, Clay and Sally Clarkson's latest endeavor offers thought-provoking insights and reflections on their parenting journey. Moms and dads can mutually benefit from the reminder that passing along the gospel to their children isn't about following a formula but about a parent's authentic relationship with God overflowing into every aspect of family life. Part handbook, part manifesto, this book offers ideas for actionable steps to nurture our children's hearts, warming them to the life-giving love of Christ.

> LAURA WIFLER AND EMILY JENSEN, cohosts of the *Risen Motherhood* podcast

Clay and Sally have once again delivered a book that every parent would be wise to read. Inviting and encouraging, this book is a tool kit for passing on an inheritance of following Christ. It's a guide for guides, teeming with wisdom earned from years of navigating the wilderness in search of the Water of Life. For the millions of younger parents longing for wise and practical mentors, *The Lifegiving Parent* is an answer to prayer.

> S. D. SMITH, author of The Green Ember series

Parenthood is an incredible gift and an extraordinary journey of discovery. *The Lifegiving Parent* is an inspirational and insightful book for all parents, no matter where they are on the journey. Each chapter is thought provoking and will challenge you as a parent to acknowledge and pursue the God-given role and influence you have in the lives of your children.

> **JENNIFER SMITH**, author of *The Unveiled Wife: Embracing Intimacy with God and Your Husband* and *Thirty-One Prayers for My Husband: Seeing God Move in His Heart*

Wisdom is crammed into these pages—the wisdom of the Scriptures exposited and the wisdom of God embodied in over three decades of parenting. You won't find formulas, guarantees, or glossy depictions of family life in this book. Instead, there are well-worn and well-loved pathways into the life-giving work of the Holy Spirit . . . for parents and for children.

> **GLENN PACKIAM**, associate senior pastor, New Life Church, Colorado Springs, and author of *Discover the Mystery of Faith: How Worship Shapes Believing*

Last year when I was in Colorado for a concert, Clay and Sally Clarkson had me over for dinner. Two of the (grown) Clarkson kids were home at the time, and the family conversation was so rich and the atmosphere so warm that I called my husband that night and told him I had just been invited into something truly remarkable. Now having read *The Lifegiving Parent*, I understand that I was enjoying the fruit of many years of intentional, Spirit-infused cultivation. In their book, the Clarksons openhandedly and systematically share the major tenants of their approach, casting an extraordinary vision of family life while somehow demystifying it at the same time. I am grateful for the generosity poured out by Clay and Sally in these pages, and I will be giving this book to all the parents I know.

> **CAROLYN ARENDS**, recording artist, author, and Renovaré director of education

It's no secret that Clay's and Sally's hearts beat for the family, and now they've offered those heartbeats for us to consider, emulate, and find encouragement from. The Clarksons specialize in inspiring a biblical big-picture mind-set with next-step practicality in a world that often finds parenting burdensome. *The Lifegiving Parent* offers delight and wonder to parents in the trenches.

> RUTH CHOU SIMONS, mom of six, founder of GraceLaced.com, artist, and bestselling author of *GraceLaced: Discovering Timeless Truths through Seasons of the Heart*

American parents often say they feel powerless to raise their kids in the best way. Either they feel inadequate to do the job or they worry they don't have the kind of influence on their kids they once dreamed of having. The solution isn't "education" as we typically think of it, nor is it slightly better sermons or youth groups. Children need *formation*—something that's far more broad, intentional, and rooted in the people and traditions that ground a home.

At a time when the plethora of parenting books are mainly focused on technique, Clay and Sally Clarkson provide a vision of parenting as an art. *The Lifegiving Parent* is an intensely practical window into how to be the person your children need so that they can grow up surrounded by the truth, goodness, and beauty that will set them up for a life worth living.

> BRIAN BROWN, director, the Anselm Society

My husband and I passed this book back and forth with enthusiasm. *The Lifegiving Parent* is for every hopeful, weary mother or father. Our home is different because of the ministry of Sally and Clay Clarkson. Their vision has lifted our eyes, and this book is a gem we'll return to again and again.

> SARA HAGERTY, grateful mother of six and author of *Unseen: The Gift of Being Hidden in a World that Loves to Be Noticed* and *Every Bitter Thing Is Sweet: Tasting the Goodness of God in All Things*

The Lifegiving Parent is for parents who want to raise children in a joy-filled home where each person is celebrated and where God is glorified. If parenting feels burdensome and creating a beautiful family culture feels out of reach, this is the book for you.

> SARAH MACKENZIE, author of *The Read-Aloud Family: Making Meaningful and Lasting Connections with Your Kids* and host of the *Read-Aloud Revival* podcast

Clay's and Sally's amazing relational styles inspire parents to new heights. They not only tell us "what" but also show us "how." Any parents who read this book will find tools to breathe new life into their homes.

> DR. SCOTT TURANSKY, author of *Parenting Is Heart Work* and cofounder of the National Center for Biblical Parenting

Clay and Sally Clarkson are the beloved parenting guides we all seek—gentle yet firm, wise yet adventurous, curious yet convicted. In *The Lifegiving Parent*, the Clarksons faithfully lead us all into a deeper, more meaningful exploration of Christian parenting through personal lessons, biblical insights, and practical teachings. To read this book is to sit down to a treasured mentorship, Yorkshire Tea in hand.

> ERIN LOECHNER, blogger at DesignForMankind.com and author of *Chasing Slow: Courage to Journey Off the Beaten Path*

There's nothing I want more than to be a life-giving parent to my children. This book is at the top of my go-to stack of books to help me through the beautiful and challenging phases and stages of parenting. You *must* add it to yours.

> KRISTEN WELCH, author of the bestselling book *Raising Grateful Kids in an Entitled World: How One Family Learned that Saying No Can Lead to Life's Biggest Yes*

THE *Life* GIVING PARENT

GIVING YOUR CHILD
a life worth living for Christ

CLAY & SALLY CLARKSON

The nonfiction imprint of
Tyndale House Publishers, Inc.

Visit Tyndale online at www.tyndale.com.

Visit Tyndale Momentum online at www.tyndalemomentum.com.

Visit Clay Clarkson at www.wholeheart.org.

Visit Sally Clarkson at www.sallyclarkson.com, www.momheart.com, and www.wholeheart.org.

TYNDALE, Tyndale Momentum, and Tyndale's quill logo are registered trademarks of Tyndale House Publishers, Inc. The Tyndale Momentum logo is a trademark of Tyndale House Publishers, Inc. Tyndale Momentum is the nonfiction imprint of Tyndale House Publishers, Inc., Carol Stream, Illinois.

The Lifegiving Parent: Giving Your Child a Life Worth Living for Christ

Designed by Julie Chen

Unless otherwise indicated, all Scripture quotations are taken from the New American Standard Bible,® copyright © 1960, 1962, 1963, 1968, 1971, 1972, 1973, 1975, 1977, 1995 by The Lockman Foundation. Used by permission.

Scripture quotations marked ESV are taken from *The Holy Bible*, English Standard Version® (ESV®), copyright © 2001 by Crossway, a publishing ministry of Good News Publishers. Used by permission. All rights reserved.

Scripture quotations marked NIV are taken from the Holy Bible, *New International Version,*® *NIV.*® Copyright © 1973, 1978, 1984, 2011 by Biblica, Inc.® (Some quotations may be from the earlier NIV edition, copyright © 1984.) Used by permission. All rights reserved worldwide.

Scripture quotations marked KJV are taken from the *Holy Bible*, King James Version.

Scripture quotations marked NLT are taken from the *Holy Bible*, New Living Translation, copyright © 1996, 2004, 2015 by Tyndale House Foundation. Used by permission of Tyndale House Publishers, Inc., Carol Stream, Illinois 60188. All rights reserved.

Scripture quotations marked NET© are used by permission and taken from the NET Bible,® copyright © 1996–2006 by Biblical Studies Press, L.L.C., http://netbible.com. All rights reserved.

For information about special discounts for bulk purchases, please contact Tyndale House Publishers at csresponse@tyndale.com, or call 1-800-323-9400.

Library of Congress Cataloging-in-Publication Data
Names: Clarkson, Clay, author.
Title: The lifegiving parent : giving your child a life worth living for Christ / Clay and Sally Clarkson.
Description: Carol Stream, Illinois : Tyndale House Publishers, Inc., 2018. | Includes bibliographical references.
Identifiers: LCCN 2017057094| ISBN 9781496431639 (hc) | ISBN 9781496421975 (sc)
Subjects: LCSH: Parenting—Religious aspects—Christianity. | Child rearing—Religious aspects—Christianity. | Christian education of children.
Classification: LCC BV4529 .C5353 2018 | DDC 248.8/45—dc23 LC record available at https://lccn.loc.gov/2017057094

Printed in the United States of America

24 23 22 21 20 19 18
7   6   5   4   3   2   1

We dedicate this book to our four wonderful children.
We gave you a life worth living for Christ, and you've made
our lives worth living. May the life of God you found in
our lifegiving home be the life that fills your own.

Contents

Foreword

Sally

SUMMER EVENINGS IN COLORADO often find us on our back deck as the sun sets behind the foothills of the Rockies. There's something about a cool breeze and gently swaying pine trees that is both rejuvenating and calming at the same time. Dare I say that it feels lifegiving? If so, then perhaps it pictures, just a little, what I hope our children have found in the life of our home and in the gentle breeze of the life of God blowing through it.

Every August, near our wedding anniversary, we gather with our children for our annual Family Day. After a full day of traditional activities, we typically end up sitting around the table on the deck, sipping a variety of beverages and enjoying those lifegiving mountain breezes. We joke and jest, converse and contend, and reminisce and remember. With four thoughtful and opinionated millennial children, there is never (ever!) a letup in the discussion. It's a Clarkson family moment.

After our last Family Day, when Clay and I had some time to be alone, we talked about that table full of blessing and destiny. Solomon was certainly right when he said in Psalm 127 that "children are a gift of the LORD"—our children have been God's gift to us in more ways than we can describe, and they will be God's gift to the world through us in ways we have yet to know, or perhaps never will know while we're still around. As we thought back together about each child around that table, we realized that in the same way we tried to give life to them in our home while they were growing up, they have given more life to us than we can measure. Lifegiving has been a two-way path.

After thirty-three years of parenting, our four delightful children are all grown and out of the house now (except when they're not). As much as we miss them, it means Clay and I have reached that pivotal parental point of being able to look back and reflect on our parenting journey—all the challenges, choices, chuckles, and changes. Since we're still involved parents to our grown children, we look back not so much with nostalgia as with contemplation. What did we do right? Where did we go wrong? What would we do differently if we could? What have we learned? What can we share with those who come behind us, whether our own children or new generations of parents? This book arose out of discussions like those.

As we talked about the stories and our years of parenting together, we understood that we, like most parents, had little conception when we started the journey what we were doing, and even less what it would require of us. We agreed that parenting was the best of all the ministry we've done in our lives, but we had no idea what that investment in our children would cost us physically, emotionally, spiritually, and financially. It is only now that we can begin to observe the dividends. Whatever lifegiving we did is now paying out in the rich life of faith we see in each of our children.

However, did I also mention the speed bumps, potholes, blind curves, and other road hazards we encountered along the path of parenting? It was not a smooth ride. After all, every Christian family, ours included, is inhabited by sinful, selfish human beings called parents and children. The idea that Christian parenting should be a purely joyful journey through life is misguided at best and an illusion at worst. And yet, despite our own immaturities and weaknesses, we made it through with no casualties and with faith intact. We're all stronger than when we started.

But Christian parenting is more than just getting from one point to another by faith. We know intuitively we're made for something more than just crossing the finish line. We're made to be part of God's epic story of creation—the story He is writing not only for all of life but for each of our lives. As lifegiving parents, one of our most important tasks has been to help our children discover themselves in the story God is writing, to find their places in the unfolding tale of God's grand purpose and plan and to know that we are all, as a family, in that story together.

As I've partnered with Clay in that bigger picture, it has been my privilege to do my best to be a godly mother to our children—to nurture their faith through my love, grace, discipleship, encouragement, instruction, and inspiration. I have found purpose and meaning in trying to be the kind of mother I believe was in God's heart at creation—a lifegiving mother, one who brings the life of God to my children. I won't pretend it was always a wonderful journey with no difficulties, but the blessings far outweigh the burdens as I see now the influences of my life on each of my children. They are, as God promised, the blessings.

For twenty years, I taught and encouraged Christian mothers in more than sixty Mom Heart Conferences to become that kind of "mother after God's heart." And there was one question that came up over and over after every event: "Does Clay have a book for dads about what you're teaching that I can give to my husband?" As a gifted teacher and seminary graduate, Clay always wanted to get to that book, but events and ministry administration would never allow enough time to write it. Now that we've retired from regular conference ministry, Clay has finally been able to carve out enough time to think about this book and write it. *The Lifegiving Parent* is the answer to that question asked by so many moms.

I had already written *The Lifegiving Home* (with our daughter Sarah) and *The Lifegiving Table*, so when Clay suggested the idea of *The Lifegiving Parent*, I was thrilled. It would not only complete a "Lifegiving" trilogy but would also finally provide the book that all those moms for so many years had been asking for—and not just for their husbands but for themselves as well. It pulls together many of the messages we've taught through the years into a book that couples can read together to shape a philosophy of how to give their children the life of God in their homes. It's not just about giving your children a Christian life but also about giving them the life of Christ. That's what it means to be a lifegiving parent.

If you want to feel that cool breeze of God's life blowing through your home and family, I pray this book will show you how to make that happen. It's not a formula but simply a way of life and faith—it's a lifegiving heart and mind-set. I'm excited for you as you read this book, not just because of what it will do for your family today but also because God's life coming alive in your home can shape generations to come through your children and their children. Lifegiving parenting will help you and your children to find yourselves in God's epic story—and to live the story He is writing through and for you.

Preface
Clay

SALLY AND I BARELY HAD TURNED the page on our first decade of marriage, and we had moved by faith to Nashville, Tennessee, just the year before. We were still feeling our way forward with three children under eight years old when the "blizzards" hit. They changed our lives.

The first blizzard was a life-threatening miscarriage for Sally. It was a disruptive reminder of the fragility of life and caused us to begin reevaluating our hopes and dreams. The second blizzard was the unexpected loss of a church staff position, forcing us to begin thinking about our future and ministry beyond Nashville. The third was, quite literally, a blizzard—the March 1993 "Storm of the Century" that paralyzed the southeast corner of the country. We had driven to Atlanta for a weekend to speak on parenting, but we ended up immobilized for four days in a small house with other speakers. That blizzard would figuratively blow us out of Tennessee three weeks later to start a new life and ministry in Texas.

Since our marriage ten years before those blizzards, I had completed seminary; we had spent three somewhat-turbulent years in international ministry with a church in Vienna, Austria; and then we had settled into a Southern California church ministry upon our return. Four years later, a church merger and building program forced a last-in-first-out staff turnover that precipitated our decision to move to Nashville, where I hoped to pitch some songs to Christian publishers. Two years—and minimal song success—later, we were in a snowbound house in Atlanta discussing the question "What would you do if you could do anything?" with other marooned visionary leaders and speakers. And just a few days later, back in Nashville, a neighbor from down the street came to our door and asked if he could buy our house and take possession in two weeks. Life moves fast in a blizzard.

When we turned off the engines of the two large U-Haul trucks two weeks later in front of my family home in rural central Texas, we stepped with trepidation into our answer to the question we'd discussed in Atlanta—if we could, we would start a ministry to help Christian parents raise godly children. That answer was not just a visionary ideal: We had already tried our hand with a parenting workshop in Nashville (maybe a dozen people attended), envisioned starting Family Faith Ministries (it never caught on), and even pitched a parenting book proposal to a major Christian publisher in Nashville (it went nowhere). Despite those three swings and misses, our flailing efforts would become a seed of experience that we would plant in Texas. One year later it would sprout and become Whole Heart Ministries.

Fast-forward twenty-five years. With God's help, we've accomplished our "what would you do if" answer to that blizzard-induced question—built an international ministry to Christian parents; spoken at countless workshops and events; sponsored more than sixty two-day motherhood conferences; written more than twenty parenting books; started an international small-groups ministry for mothers; and built an online ministry reaching tens of thousands. We're most grateful to have raised four children who now, as adults, love and follow the Lord with a heart for ministry. (You'll read more about them throughout the book.)

As parents of adult children now, we're slowing down and once more taking stock of our lives for the new journey ahead. If there is a blizzard stirring up that process for us, it's the uncertain winds of time and change (which, of course, are always blowing for everyone, but become more brisk the further along we are on the journey). The question we ask is no longer just what would we do if we could, but also what have we done. What have we learned in twenty-five years of parenting ministry that can help a new generation of moms and dads raise "wholehearted" Christian children? It seems like the right time to revisit the paths, practices, and truths that have defined our ministry over the years—not just the ones that have lasted the longest, but the ones that have become stronger the longer we've walked with them on our journey of Christian parenting.

Sally and Sarah (our oldest child) recently wrote *The Lifegiving Home,* and Sally followed that up with *The Lifegiving Table.* Both books look back on how we worked out what God had worked into our hearts over our years of parenting—and how it affected our children's hearts. The first examines the spiritual influence of home traditions, and the second focuses on the family table. The book you now hold in your hand—*The Lifegiving Parent*—completes a "Lifegiving" trilogy of books that look back into our family experience with a life-colored perspective on what we learned from Scripture, from our children, and from our unusual and unexpected adventures in Christian parenting.

Like Sally's two other "lifegiving" books, *The Lifegiving Parent* is a big-picture overview, not just of what worked pragmatically for us but also of what worked spiritually. It's not your typical book containing primarily how-to and what-to-do parenting wisdom, or a doctrinal survey and commentary of Bible verses on parenting, or a special model of biblical parenting. There's nothing inherently wrong with any of those approaches, all of which are represented in this book, as long as they don't promise unqualified parenting success if you use them. This book does not. However, at the heart of this book is a fundamental truth I think many Christian parenting books might overlook—the life of God.

This is a book about what Sally and I did to bring God's life into our home for our children to see and believe. That's what it means to be a lifegiving parent—to introduce our children to the living God of Scripture and to give them the life that we have found in Him. We offer no special or secret formula that will make you a successful Christian parent, and we would counsel you to avoid any parenting book that does. We offer only our personal experiences and insights, and the promise that God's grace will be in abundant supply for anything you decide to do by faith in order to become a lifegiving parent for your children. That will be the real story of this book—how God comes alive in your family.

And here's the rest of my story about this book. As Sally was writing *The Lifegiving Home* and *The Lifegiving Table*, I suggested to her that perhaps I should write a book about lifegiving parenting. After all, it was a good concept, it would make a nice trilogy of books, and it would be an opportunity to summarize the convictions and insights about biblical parenting that had fueled our ministry for a quarter century. But since it was a new concept for me, I would need a strong outline before I could take it to our publisher. I found myself in a deep dive into my research files.

As I slogged through hundreds of pages of old notes, messages, outlines, and documents, I found at the very back of one rarely opened file drawer a manila folder labeled simply "Book Proposal." I opened it and quickly realized what I had found—it was the filed-away and forgotten book proposal dating from that year of blizzards in Nashville. My very first (and not very good) book proposal. Perhaps I should not have been surprised at the working title of that first book concept, but I was momentarily stunned when I saw "The Lifegiving Parent." I had absolutely no recollection of it having ever been a book I had conceived, much less proposed, but there it was, pushing its way back into the present, inviting itself back into my mind after all these years.

As I read the twenty-five-year-old outline, I was taken aback that the concepts it expressed were ones we are still teaching and championing today. We're more confident and have much more to say now—the maturity that comes from both success and failure has added breadth and depth to our early ideas and ideals—but the path of parenting we started on is the same path we're still on. We've changed and grown, but the truths of God's Word and His wisdom for parents have stayed the same. You might say the past is always present for God. It took only a short time to edit that early outline, expand and craft its formative ideas, and turn it into a new proposal for this book.

Perhaps this brief backstory will remind you that divine truths, though they may be hidden by time and circumstances, don't really change—they are simply waiting to be found and appreciated again, maybe even leaving us a little stunned that we ever forgot or overlooked them in the first place. In this book, I hope to uncover some of those truths about bringing the life of God into our homes, discovering their surprising currency for our parenting today. After all, God has revealed Himself to us as a heavenly parent, so some concepts of parenting are not only taught in His Word but are also eternal and implanted in our own spirits by the image of God that we bear. It is my hope that this book will invite those parenting truths into your present, to resonate with your heart and come alive in your home.

The goal of this book is very simple: to inspire and encourage you to become a lifegiving parent who invites the living God of eternity into your home and family. In chapter 1, we'll look at the countercultural nature of lifegiving parenting and the critical importance of imparting God's life to our children. In chapters 2–9, we'll look at eight specific "Heartbeats of Parental Lifegiving" that characterize the ways we can bring God's life into our homes to give to our children. Our family's stories and insights will provide illustrative stepping-stones, and selected Bible passages will provide divine directions for moving forward. Each heartbeat chapter will end with one of "Sally's Lifegiving Momoirs," a personal story from her parenting journey as a mother; "Lifegiving ParenTips," three personal and practical ways to respond to each heartbeat; and "Starting the Heartbeat of Parental Lifegiving," a one-sentence recap of the chapter's message along with an action step you can take to implement lifegiving parenting. In chapter 10, we'll look ahead to the end of the journey to find motivation for becoming a lifegiving parent. We all have only "one life to give" for our children, so we need to make sure it's one that will indeed give them life. Finally, the epilogue will provide a brief look into "Our Lifegiving Parent Story," a glance at where our parenting journey has taken Sally and me and our children in this life with God.

Sally and I hope that the concept of lifegiving parenting can be a parental paradigm shift for you, a new way of thinking about raising your children to know and follow Christ. Our prayer is that rather than being overwhelmed, you will sense a new freedom by discovering a different way of life at home with your children. As you read each chapter, please don't get hung up on the specifics of what we did or what you need to accomplish in your home. At its core, lifegiving parenting is less about what you do and more about who you are— a child of the living God who is connected with Him and is ready to share that life with your children so that they may know Him too.

What we share in this book has grown out of our own story, but it can also become the words and ways that will help you write your own story—the story of a Christian home alive with the life of God, the story of children finding their lives in the God they see and experience there through the faith of their parents, and the story of faith and hope in the God of life that—because of you—will go from your home into the world and into future generations. No matter what your family looks like, what you've done, where you've come from, or where you are in life right now, you can become a lifegiving parent. You can learn to bring the life of God into your home, to give His life to your children, and to find even more of His life for yourself in the process. It's not a foolproof formula to follow; it's a life of faith to live and to give. Join us on the journey of becoming a lifegiving parent.

CHAPTER I

SOMEONE'S GOT TO GIVE

Thus says the LORD, "Stand by the ways and see and ask for the ancient paths, where the good way is, and walk in it; and you will find rest for your souls."
JEREMIAH 6:16

FAMILY IS CHANGING. Anyone who has lived through the last few decades of American life has watched that change move like a prairie storm across the landscape of our culture—sometimes slowly, sometimes swiftly, but always with steady, inevitable progress. Nothing is quite the same in the wake of a cultural storm's winds and rains. When it hits where you live, change happens. And it's happening now to home and family.

If a movie can be like a parable of Jesus, I'd have to suggest that the 1939 classic *The Wizard of Oz* comes close as a cinematic parable of our current experience. The movie begins in black and white, with young Dorothy Gale living a simple life anchored in the abiding fundamentals of family and faithfulness and surrounded by the unchanging stability of the Kansas prairie. But then a raging cyclone transports her farmhouse—with Dorothy and her little black dog, Toto, inside—to a new and unfamiliar, but very colorful, place. As she wanders along a yellow-bricked path outside her relocated house, taking in the strangeness of all she is seeing in the yet-unnamed Land of Oz, she voices the obvious: "Toto, I've a feeling we're not in Kansas anymore."

Over the last generation, a storm has blown across our Christian cultural landscape with the ferocity of a Kansas tornado. It picked up our values of home and family and carried them and us to a new place that is strange and unsettling. Like Dorothy, we're wandering along a well-trodden path to the Great and Mighty One, trying to make sense of the new world we see around us. And in our hearts, despite the changes we're experiencing, we still believe, like Dorothy, "There's no place like home."

Change is a reality of life that we can resist but can't avoid. And yet while things are changing all around us, the *kinds* of changes we see—the big, global changes that we call human progress—remain the same from generation to generation. Solomon, as king of Israel, changed that land like no one before him or since—he built the Temple, enlarged its treasures, made Israel a nation among nations, and transformed Jerusalem into a world-class city. And yet he wrote in Ecclesiastes 1:9, "That which has been is that which will be, and that which has been done is that which will be done. So there is nothing new under the sun." Solomon was enlarging his domain and influence as countless other kingdoms and governments have done. The details may differ, but we as humans keep doing the same things, in the same ways, with the same good—and bad—intentions and outcomes. That's the paradox, and in part the message of Ecclesiastes: The world changes, but humans remain the same.

We're naturally fascinated by the big, culture-defining changes of the kind that Solomon ushered in for Israel—changes in society, industry, commerce, education, governance, technology, fashion, leisure, and other areas. But most of us, as believers in Jesus and His teachings, don't really change inside when things change around us—we still want the fundamental human values and virtues we believe in to remain the same. Whatever else is changing, we expect foundational biblical truths to stay firm. It's an article of our faith. But now that's being challenged too.

⚜

The cultural changes we're seeing in our current time "under the sun," not just in matters of home and family but also in attitudes toward Christian truth and morality, are of the fundamental kind, the ones we couldn't or didn't want to see coming but that now we cannot avoid—shifting attitudes about sexuality and marriage, the prevalence of divorce and fragmentation of families, conflicting ideas about God, challenges to the Bible's authority, rejection of once widely held Christian standards and beliefs. We're seeing increasingly dramatic confrontations over some of God's foundational "solid rock" truths that provide stability and safety from the storms of life. Even though we as believers are building our homes "on the rock" of Jesus' words, more and more homes built "on the sand" surround us and are vulnerable to the storms (see Matthew 7:24-27). Sandy foundations for many are being eroded and washed away.

David asks in one of his psalms, "If the foundations are destroyed, what can the righteous do?" (11:3). It's a good question. What happens when the foundations change? What is our response when our fundamental values are no longer honored? What do we do when the foundations we live by are rejected by those around us, or even by our country? Or when rulers over us do not affirm or protect our cherished ways of life as Christians? As a psalmist of Israel, David's answer was a simple reminder of what followers of God have always known to do—to trust God because He reigns from His temple in heaven and will protect the righteous (see 11:4, 7). As king of Israel, though, David could not foresee what his question perhaps presciently foreshadowed for the future of his country.

About four hundred years after David's reign as God's king over all Israel, the ancient foundations of the Promised Land, already split into two kingdoms, were being further decimated—the northern kingdom of Israel had already been conquered and scattered by Assyria, and the southern kingdom of Judah (the land of Jerusalem and the Temple) was less than a decade from being overthrown and exiled to Babylon for seventy years. In the midst of all that change and many prophecies of coming judgment, God offered an indirect answer to David's Psalm 11:3 question through Jeremiah, a prophet to Judah: "Thus says the LORD, 'Stand by the ways and see and ask for the ancient paths, where the good way is, and walk in it; and you will find rest for your souls'" (Jeremiah 6:16).

When the foundations and fundamentals of Christianity that have provided stability for us for so long are rocked by challenge and change, and Kansas seems like a distant memory, the answer is not to panic, or fight, or just give up. The answer is, in fact, to be like Dorothy in Oz—to adjust and adapt, keep going, keep believing, and never give up the vision of home. The biblical answer to David's question, and to ours, is to trust that the God we know is faithful and the ancient paths we know are good. In other words, when things are changing around us, we stay faithful and stay the course. In that path alone we'll find peace in the midst of conflict.

Whatever else we may do in response to the changes happening around us, the one thing we cannot do is neglect our families. The eight heartbeats of lifegiving parenting covered in chapters 2–9 are an attempt to define, at least in part, what "the good way" will be for serious Christian families to walk in as we navigate through our uncertain time "under the sun." It's not just about being a "good Christian family" as a testimony to the world, or about combating the growing decline of the biblical family in our culture. It's about something much more important—it's about bringing your children into contact with the living God whom you serve so they will want to serve Him too. It's about your children finding life in God so they can stay faithful to the faith you pass on to them.

〰 〰

In the same way that the nation of Israel changed dramatically over its first four hundred years, so have American culture and Christianity. The purpose of this book is not to address those changes, and it is especially not to try to redress them. Instead, I want to speak to Christian families who are committed to building the kind of homes that can withstand the storms of culture blowing in with those changes—the kind of lifegiving homes Jesus said are built on the rock of His Word (see Matthew 7:24-27).

Lifegiving parenting is not about changing the culture we live in but about being a counterculture to it. It's not about creating a comfortable Christian subculture insulated from the surrounding world; rather, it's about being the kind of lifegiving home culture that will stand as a testimony of God's biblical design for family to a lost world whose sandy foundations are washing away. It's not about being a political or social "culture warrior" for the family but about definitively, and maybe even defiantly, building a home where the living God of Creation is undeniably living through the family within it. Lifegiving parenting is about bringing the life of God into your home and family to create, with Him, an outpost of the Kingdom of Heaven in this world. We can call that place a "Christian home," but Christians often have very different ideas of what those words mean.

Throughout the quarter century of what I call our Christian home and parenting ministry, we've met and seen many families with life-affirming and life-infused Christian homes, where the presence of God was unmistakable in the parents' vision for their biblical roles and in the spiritual homelife they were cultivating for their children. However, we've also observed many American Christian families where the parents, though unquestionably believers, seemed minimally engaged in the spiritual life of the home or their children. If asked to give a rea-son why theirs was a Christian home, they might answer by focusing mostly on what their children were doing—"My kids go to church, Sunday School, Bible club, youth group, and camp; have all the best Christian music, videos, books, and apps; attend a Christian school; go to VBS and Christian activities; and have great Christian friends. Of course they're being raised in a Christian home."

There's no question that exposing children to so many good and godly Christian influences can be a positive thing. However, it can also become a negative thing if Christian consumerism becomes either an unintentional or preferred substitute for the life of God in a family. We need to distinguish between a home that is considered Christian primarily because cultural Christianity happens there and a home that is Christian because Christ is alive and present in percep-tible ways. Here's the reality that needs to be affirmed: A distinctively Christian home can never be defined only by what the children are doing; it must be defined by what the parents are doing.

Despite what the pervasive Christian culture many of us live in may lead you to believe, no amount of Christian activities, materials, or media for your children will be able to make your home a Christian home. Those can all be good, edifying, enjoyable, and fun for your family, but they are powerless in themselves to bring the life of God into your home. Only you—parents alive in Christ because of the Holy Spirit within you—have the ability and the power of the Spirit to make your home a Christian home. Engagement with Christian culture does not define a Christian home; engagement with the living Christ does. That understanding is a necessary first step on the path to becoming a lifegiving parent.

❧ ☙

This is where authors often cite statistics to bolster their arguments. However, while statistics can legitimately tell a story that engages our minds and hearts, they can also be misused to portray a crisis that we need to fear. Data can be misinterpreted or misunderstood. For example, during the 2000s, many Christian parents were confronted with shockingly dire statistics about Christian youth abandoning the church and their faith as they entered college and early adulthood. Some youth ministries used those statistics to convince parents of the critical need for their programs. Those "scare-tistics" were sometimes exaggerated and misquoted and were later challenged by better research and data, but there was no way to undo their impact.

But here's a different kind of statistical story, a better one that captures our hearts and minds without fear. For nearly forty years, Vern Bengtson and his colleagues conducted a multigenerational study of religion and family—the largest such study ever done. It followed 350 extended families representing more than 3,500 individuals whose birth dates spanned more than a century. In his book about the study, *Families and Faith: How Religion Is Passed Down across Generations*, Bengtson's top three conclusions tell a better story: "Religious families are surprisingly successful at transmission. . . . Parental influence has not declined since the 1970s. . . . Parental warmth is the key to successful transmission."[1]

The real story that parents need to hear in these times is that in spite of the season of epic change in which we find ourselves, the fundamentals of faith transmission and retention within families have not really changed. Even though we're going through yet another generational transition, with new technologies and mobile communication radically reshaping the cultural landscape in which our children and youth will grow up and find their way, the research confirms that faith is still passed along in families the same way as it always has been—through parents. And Bengtson's conclusions are remarkably consistent with a 3,500-year-old biblical model that still works for passing faith from one generation to the next. The story of that "statistic" should engage your heart and mind.

⤳ ⤲

Perhaps you've heard the term *shema*, but you don't know where it's from or what it means. You're probably not alone. It's simply the Hebrew word for "hear," but it is the first word of what Jews consider the most important passage of Holy Scripture. The verses are called the Shema and have been recited twice daily (at morning and evening prayers) by pious Jews since they were first spoken by Moses:

> Hear, O Israel! The LORD is our God, the LORD is one!
> You shall love the LORD your God with all your heart and
> with all your soul and with all your might. These words,
> which I am commanding you today, shall be on your heart.
> You shall teach them diligently to your sons and shall talk
> of them when you sit in your house and when you walk
> by the way and when you lie down and when you rise up.
> You shall bind them as a sign on your hand and they shall
> be as frontals on your forehead. You shall write them on
> the doorposts of your house and on your gates.
>
> DEUTERONOMY 6:4-9

There are other important passages for Jews, and the full Shema includes two additional passages (Deuteronomy 11:13-21 and Numbers 15:37-41), but this initial passage of the Shema Yisra'el ("Hear, O Israel") has given Jews an identity as a people who name the Lord as their God (vv. 4-5), who tell their children about their God (v. 7), and who make their God a part of their lives and homes (vv. 8-9). Throughout the storied history of the Jews, the Shema has held them together.

It helps to remember the stories that lead up to this passage. After the flood of Noah, the story of the people and nation of Israel begins with God's call to Abraham (then called Abram) to leave the land of Ur, and His promise to give him a land and raise up a people from his seed. Abraham's late-in-life son, Isaac, has a son, Jacob, who wrestles with God and is given the name Israel. He has twelve sons who eventually become patriarchs of the twelve tribes of Israel, which are named after them. At age seventeen, the youngest son, Joseph, is sold by his jealous brothers into slavery in Egypt. Joseph rises from prisoner to prominence in Egypt and saves his family from famine by moving them there from Canaan.

Though Joseph saves his family, their move to Egypt results in four hundred years of captivity for the rapidly multiplying Hebrew people, forced to serve as slaves to the Egyptians. Their exile ends when God raises up Moses to free His people from slavery. The Israelites pass through the parted Red Sea and receive at Mount Sinai the Law they would need to become a nation, but then they succumb to fear and unbelief and fail to enter the Promised Land. After wandering for forty years in the wilderness, Moses and the people finally come to the Jordan River and look across into the land God promised their forefather Abraham five hundred years earlier. They are finally about to become a nation.

Now imagine what Moses is thinking. He knows he will not be able to cross the Jordan to enter the Promised Land (see Numbers 20:8-12), and he knows his visionary leadership of the people will pass to his faithful aide, Joshua, a military man of action. On the east side of the river, Moses has gathered all the people together to encourage them and remind them of who they are—not escaped slaves from Egypt but the children of Abraham and the people of God. He wants to remind them of all that God has done to bring them to this point, read the Law that God gave him on Mount Sinai, and prepare them to become a nation.

In his 120 years of living, Moses has been many men: a prince of Egypt in Pharaoh's house; the runaway Hebrew slave who became a shepherd, husband, and father in Midian; the reluctant leader

God speaks to from the burning bush, calling him to set His people free; the returned leader of the Hebrews who would, through God's might, neutralize the vast power of Egypt with ten plagues and lead His people to freedom; the divider of the Red Sea; and the receiver of the Ten Commandments and the Law directly from God. Moses is feeling the weight of all that history and the responsibility he has carried so long for this people. Every word he speaks will be critical. This is his last opportunity to teach them "the commandment, the statutes and the judgments which the LORD your God has commanded" (Deuteronomy 6:1). This is his last time to set their courses for the future before they enter the Promised Land.

Moses addresses the assembled tribes of Israel not just as individuals but also as families—"so that you and your son and your grandson might fear the LORD your God" (v. 2). Implicit in his address is his conviction that the family will be key to the future survival and success of the nation of Israel. In the season of epic change that Israel is about to endure, Moses doubles down on the fundamentals—worship only God (v. 4), love God completely (v. 5), learn God's commandments (v. 6), teach them to your children (v. 7), and keep God alive in your home (vv. 8-9).

First, Moses proclaims that the Lord will be the Israelites' God. Other Canaanite and pagan nations surrounding them will have their Baals and other false gods, usually many of them, but the Lord is the one true God, and the Israelites are to worship Him alone, keeping the first of the Ten Commandments—"You shall have no other gods before Me" (5:7). Then Moses exhorts them that they are to love the Lord their God with all their hearts, souls, and might—totally, without reservation, with pure and complete trust, with their entire being. Jesus would consider the combination of these first two statements of belief and devotion to be the great and foremost commandment of the Law (see Matthew 22:36-38). It is important to remember that Moses has just indicated (6:2-3) that he is directing

SOMEONE'S GOT TO GIVE ⚹ 11

his words especially to parents, so this part of the Shema is also arguably the starting point for all good parenting, whether 3,500 years
ago or today. *Christian* parenting, then, must also start with the Lord,
the one God we believe in and love with all that we are, who was
incarnated for us in Jesus, our Savior.

Next, Moses tells the Israelites that all the commandments he
is teaching them ("these words") are to be first on their hearts. It's
not just about mental assent or head knowledge but is also about
assimilating his teaching so that it will change their very beings. And
then he specifically addresses the parents again, telling them they are
to teach what is now on their hearts to their children ("sons") and
that teaching is not to be done passively and casually but actively
and "diligently." He uses a word that means "to whet, or sharpen,"
suggesting that the Hebrew parents were to sharpen their children's
hearts with God's commandments and truth. And what cannot be
missed here is the truth Moses is declaring for every parent from then
until now: You cannot put into your children's hearts what is not first
in your own heart, and it will only get there through an active and
purposeful relationship with God. You are the key—truth transmission begins in your heart.

Finally, Moses turns to the family, suggesting that what happens
in parents' and children's hearts must also be reflected in the life of
the home. He uses Hebrew parallelisms—opposites that indicate a
whole—to make a clear statement about the kind of relationship that
will pass along faith and truth from parents to children. The diligent
teaching he says must happen cannot occur only when the place and
time are convenient; it is to happen everywhere ("when you sit in
your house and when you walk by the way") and all the time ("when
you lie down and when you rise up"). In other words, there is no
place and no time when teaching children about God should not be
happening. Then Moses exhorts them that the words of God must
be so clearly a part of their lives that it would be as though they were

wearing them on their bodies and displaying them on their dwellings. (While these verses sound like literal commands, other verses suggest a figurative sense to these teachings.) For parents of any era, the truth is clear—what goes into the heart must come out in a life. If we want to be lifegiving parents, there should be no question that God is alive in our hearts and homes.

⊰   ⊱

Why spend so much time on this ancient statement of faith for Israel? It's 3,500 years old! Why is it important for us now, in the midst of our season of fundamental changes? How does an ancient text relate to the idea of lifegiving parenting? Second-century apologist, theologian, and bishop Irenaeus of Lyons (France) has something to say about that: "The glory of God is a human being fully alive; and to be alive consists in beholding God." Despite the seeming circularity of his statement, Irenaeus is saying simply that we will become the "fully alive" people God designed us to be only by engaging with the living God. To put it another way, real life is found only in the life of God. That is, essentially, what I believe Moses was saying to parents in the Shema—real life is found only in God, and the life of God in our hearts must be diligently passed on to our children's hearts. Godly parenting is heart to heart, but it's also more—it's life to life. That's the relational heart of lifegiving parenting.

But don't miss a hidden-in-plain-sight truth: If lifegiving parenting is about giving our children real life in God so they can be fully alive in Him, then . . . *someone's got to give.* That transfer of the life of God to our children does not happen just by good intent or by accident. It happens for one reason only—because we decide that *we* are the people who've got to give. Not another person, group, or church; not an organization, resource, or influence . . . just us. We are the lifegivers. We are the ones who will give the life of God to our children. When we can get our heads, hearts, and hands firmly around that reality, then we'll be on the path to becoming the life-giving parents God designed us to be.

⊰ ⊱

Comments about the life of God permeate all of Scripture. It is, after all, the "living and active" Word of God (Hebrews 4:12), given life by the living God who gave it to us. In Genesis, "the LORD God formed man of dust from the ground, and breathed into his nostrils the breath of life; and man became a living being" (2:7). David wrote, "For with You is the fountain of life; in Your light we see light" (Psalm 36:9). In the first words of his Gospel, mirroring the first words of Genesis, John says of Jesus, who is God incarnate, "In Him was life, and the life was the Light of men" (John 1:4). Paul says that Jesus "abolished death and brought life and immortality to light through the gospel" (2 Timothy 1:10).

As you can see, in many passages throughout Scripture about the life of God, the light of God also shines. The first words of God are "Let there be light" (Genesis 1:3), for without light there is no life. David says, "The LORD is my light and my salvation" (Psalm 27:1), the One who saves his life. Jesus, the incarnate Son of God, proclaimed, "I am the Light of the world; he who follows Me will not walk in the darkness, but will have the Light of life" (John 8:12). In his first epistle, John says, "God is Light, and in Him there is no darkness at all" (1 John 1:5). Paul admonishes believers, "At one time you were darkness, but now you are light in the Lord. Walk as children of light" (Ephesians 5:8, ESV).

So when we give our children God's life, we are also giving them His light. It is the light of God that will shine in our hearts and our homes so that we can be a beacon of hope to the world around us. From a personal perspective as parents who love our children, life-giving parenting must first be about helping them find eternal life in Christ and getting them on God's path so they can live in a way that's pleasing to Him. That is certainly the priority of lifegiving parenting. But it is also so much more than that.

On a much grander scale, lifegiving parenting is about becoming a part of the epic story of God breaking into our dark and dying world to bring light and life. It is about writing ourselves and our children into the overarching story of God's eternal plan, "giving thanks to the Father, who has qualified us to share in the inheritance of the saints in Light. For He rescued us from the domain of darkness, and transferred us to the kingdom of His beloved Son" (Colossians 1:12-13). His life and light are what make us "the light of the world" so that we can "shine before men in such a way that they may see [our] good works, and glorify [our] Father who is in heaven" (Matthew 5:14, 16). We're turning on that light in our homes so others who are overcome by darkness and death may see it and find the life and freedom in Christ that we have found.

Lifegiving parenting is not a program to implement in your home or a set of principles and practices to say and do. It's not a formula, a ritual, or a set of rules. It is a way of living. From one perspective, it is like building and cultivating a Christian home—creating a structure and atmosphere in which the Spirit of God can work to bring the life of God to you, and through you to your children. To consider how the life of God gets into your home, I think it might be helpful to consider an illustration about a house, which has only a limited number of openings where things can come in.

The primary way the life of God gets into your home is through doors. There are numerous symbolic doors in Scripture, especially in the New Testament—doors of faith, judgment, and opportunity. Jesus calls Himself "the door" to salvation (John 10:9). But perhaps the most picturesque door is in Revelation 3:20: "Behold, I stand at the door and knock; if anyone hears My voice and opens the door, I will come in to him and will dine with him, and he with Me." Jesus is speaking to "those whom I love" (v. 19), asking if He can come in and sit down at their table with them to eat. As parents, you want to be sure that door is open in your home. It is, of course, the door to eternal life in Christ, but it is also the door to welcome the love of God in the person of Christ. Remember, too, that Jesus said, "By this all men will know that you are My disciples, if you have love for one another" (John 13:35). So keep your door open for others whom He loves and who love Him; they will bring Christ's life in with them. Lifegiving parents open the door of their homes to Christ and His followers to let the love of God in.

Another obvious way the life of God gets into your home is through windows. We don't think of windows as entries, like doors, but their purpose is no less important: Windows let in light. Thinking about our symbolic home, windows let in the light of God—His truth, grace, wisdom, hope, love, joy, peace, forgiveness, mercy, help, and so much more. Windows are where the light of God's Word enters your home as a lamp to your feet and a light to your path (see Psalm 119:105). A window lets in the light of God that "has shone in our hearts to give the Light of the knowledge of the glory of God in the face of Christ" (2 Corinthians 4:6). The more windows you have in your home—family devotions and prayers, short and long Bible readings, Scripture verses on the walls, Bibles in easy reach, talking about God at meals, sharing testimonies of His grace and help—the more the light of God can shine in. Lifegiving parents open the windows of their homes to let the light of God in.

A final way the life of God gets into your home is not quite so obvious—through vents. We don't often think about vents, but they are critical to a healthy home. In a modern home, vents work two ways—they help bring fresh, new air into a house, and they also take stale, old air out. We were reminded of the importance of vents when we had a whole-house fan that burned out twice because, as we finally learned, we didn't have enough ventilation in the attic. In our symbolic home, vents are how the life of God through the Holy

Spirit can fill your dwelling. The Greek word for "Spirit" (*pneuma*) means "breath" or "wind," and Jesus compares the Holy Spirit to wind when describing those who are "born of the Spirit" (John 3:8). Ventilation is all about the Spirit—trusting in His presence, living by faith, relying on His power, reading Scripture with His guidance, worshiping God in Spirit, asking for His wisdom. We don't often "see" the work of the Spirit, but we know it is real. He brings His new life to our spirits and removes the old life. Lifegiving parents open the vents of their homes to let the life of God in.

If you want to get to the beating heart of being a lifegiving parent, you'll find it in opening your home to the love of God, the light of God, and the life of God. If you faithfully keep the symbolic door, windows, and vents of your home open, then your house will be full of God's love, light, and life. Lifegiving parenting is all about creating a home for your children that is loving, enlightened, and alive with the presence and life of God.

❧ ❧

As I said above but need to say again, lifegiving parenting is not a formula, program, or set of rules to follow. That's not how life happens. It's simply about inviting Jesus into your home to eat at your table and be with you; pulling back any curtains of bad habits, sin, or laziness to let as much of the light of God into your home every day as you can; and opening and cleaning all the vents so the Holy Spirit can breathe and fill up the airspace of your home with His presence.

This book is an invitation to start living like a lifegiving parent. In the chapters that follow, I'll talk about eight "heartbeats" of lifegiving parenting—the kinds of biblical patterns and priorities that can help bring the life of God into your home in ways that your children can see and know are real. However, let me offer a quick disclaimer here.

This book is not a theology of parenting. Each heartbeat grows out of direct or indirect parenting passages from Scripture that I have long studied, taught, and written about. Still, the eight heartbeats are not a comprehensive biblical presentation, and others could certainly be added. The ones here, though, work together to form a complete, holistic biblical idea. You can be confident that what's covered in this book will put you on the path to becoming a lifegiving parent.

The reality is that Scripture does not provide a systematic doctrine of child raising. Instead, what we have is partial, anecdotal, and somewhat random. There are enough biblical cues and clues to discern what God wants us to know about parenting, but from my study it seems clear that He has purposely left the subject incomplete—He leaves it to our discretion to take the pieces He provides and make the whole. Why? I believe He doesn't want us enslaved by conformity to only one "right way" of child raising; he wants us free in Christ to parent in the power of the Holy Spirit by faith. Faith and freedom should be the nature of our life in the Spirit, and it should be the nature of our life at home as parents.

Perhaps you're continuing a journey you're already on and are just looking for new parenting ideas. Perhaps you're stepping onto the path of lifegiving parenting for the first time, looking for God's direction for your home. Or perhaps you're considering a new paradigm for your Christian home—moving from a legalistic model of form and function to a lifegiving model of faith and freedom. However you come to lifegiving parenting, and whatever it leads you to do in your home, keep Paul's admonition in mind: "The Lord is the Spirit, and where the Spirit of the Lord is, there is freedom" (2 Corinthians 3:17, NIV). You're free in God's Spirit to discover what is right for your home.

The world is changing around you, but it doesn't need to change you. The fundamentals of biblical parenting are the rock on which

God invites you to build your home, the foundation that will keep it safe and standing against the rains, floods, and winds of the cultural storms of change. As it was true for Dorothy, it's true for you, too—there's no place like home. As you begin the journey of lifegiving parenting, the Spirit will make sure of that.

PART I

Heartbeats of Parental Lifegiving

CHAPTER 2

NUMBERING YOUR CHILD'S DAYS

Teach us to number our days, that we may present to You a heart of wisdom.

PSALM 90:12

FAMILY PLANNING for Sally and me was never about if or when to have children, or how many to have. It was always about planning for our life as a family—what kind of parents we would be, what the Bible said to us about parenting, and how we would help our children love God. We didn't know it at the time, but our family planning would reflect Moses' heart that we learn to "number our days" (Psalm 90:12). We started out doing that just for ourselves, but we learned soon enough that our children needed us to do it for them, too. Numbering our children's days became a normal part of our family planning.

We got in the habit of numbering our days—using time well and setting goals with pleasing God in mind—right from the start as a new couple, although our personalities approached planning very differently. I'm a consummate written-list maker, which Sally finds needless and time wasting; Sally is a natural mental-list minder, which I find frustratingly unsystematic and random. Still, despite our fundamentally different and sometimes-conflicting planning tacks, we both came to marriage with an expectation of setting goals and making plans. Neither of us ever had to cajole or convince the other to plan.

During our twenties, each of us had been involved with the same national Christian ministry on different college campuses in Texas (we met at a state conference), and after graduation in 1975 we both joined the staff of that ministry (we dated at staff orientation). Whether it was due to ministry training, natural instinct, personality, or a combination of factors, we each learned by experience during our time on staff to value the discipline of planning our days, weeks, and even years.

After five years of doing ministry in different locations, we reconnected when we both landed in Denver, Colorado, and were married a year later on August 30, 1981. Our honeymoon itinerary ended in Denver, and I started classes almost immediately for my second year of MDiv studies at Denver Seminary. As we settled into our new life, we initiated a pattern of going out for a "planning breakfast" on Monday mornings. We did the requisite calendar planning, of course, but we spent most of our time talking about our spiritual lives, discussing family activities and traditions, planning our personal and shared ministries, and often engaging in longer-term planning. Of course, it was also a great way to spend time together as a new couple.

Our time as "married singles" came to an end when Sarah Elizabeth was born in 1984. We had officially become parents, but our planning pattern kept going as before, with only one "small" change—Sarah would join us on our Monday morning outings, lying quietly (usually) in her baby carrier on the floor next to our table or booth. Even though she could not yet take part in our lively planning discussions, she was nonetheless a regular topic of conversation. Her presence alone changed the focus of our planning. It was no longer just about numbering our days; it was now also about numbering her days—thinking about how we would use our time with her, what we wanted to teach her, and the goals we had for her as she grew. A new eternal soul under our care had come into our lives, and her days were in our hands.

⊰ ⊱

The first heartbeat of lifegiving parenting is numbering your child's days. It's at the top of the list of heartbeats—not because of some practical notion that planning must out of necessity precede doing, but rather out of personal conviction that vision should define direction. What you envision as a priority of your life is what will determine the direction you take. David, the greatest king of Israel, prayed, "LORD, make me to know my end and what is the extent of my days; let me know how transient I am. . . . And now, Lord, for what do I wait? My hope is in You" (Psalm 39:4, 7). Long before popular author Stephen R. Covey made the phrase popular in his book *The 7 Habits of Highly Effective People*, David had developed a "beginning with the end in mind" perspective on life. And according to David's psalm, it was God's idea to begin with.

You may be thinking, *Well, I suppose that idea works for me as an adult, but how can it work for my children? They don't understand enough about life to have that kind of perspective.* But that's precisely why it's a priority for you *for* your children. The reality is that you have only about a ten-year window with each of your children to prepare them for the remaining decades of their lives. In childhood, you can form their values, attitudes, and character; as they enter young adulthood (their teens), your influence and instruction will begin to set in their hearts and minds; as they enter adulthood, your influence lessens as who they are becomes more settled.

Sally and I have frequently talked about a ten-year period of childhood we call the four-to-fourteen window—the prime parental teaching period, starting when a child is four and ending when he or she is about fourteen. We didn't have any hard research to prove the validity of those beginning and ending ages. Rather, over our twenty-five years of parenting, it's when we observed that those heart windows were most open for each of our children. We first identified the window as an informed observation and not from Scripture study, but we learned from subsequent research that the window does have some sound biblical support as part of a consistent three-stage view of life in Scripture—childhood, young adulthood, and adulthood. (See the heading in chapter 10 titled "Know Your Child as Good.")

Because the window we call childhood is so "transient," to use David's language, we need to make the most of those years. Our children's childhoods are here and gone before we know it, and while our influence continues in young adulthood in a different way, we don't have a second chance to make a first impression on our children's hearts while that window is most divinely open to our influence. This is what Moses describes in what would come to be called the Shema, the statement of faith that has guided Israel's people and parents for more than three millennia (Deuteronomy 6:4-9; see chapter 1). That open window of childhood is when we as parents need to be thinking about "beginning with the end in mind," and how that perspective should shape our intentions for parenting our children's hearts and lives.

᪱ ᪱

If we fail to number our children's days—to be serious about how we will shape and influence their hearts and minds for God during our brief window of opportunity—then others will do that for us, with or without our consent. Our children will take from others—whether peers, culture, church, media, teachers, or strangers—the influence and instruction that God designed them to find primarily from us, their parents (see chapter 6). Our children's spirits are hardwired by God to look to us first for the spiritual influence they long for because of God's image within them. If they don't get it from us, they'll seek it elsewhere.

A closer look at Moses' prayer in Psalm 90 reinforces this idea. It is a prayer to the God who has "been our dwelling place in all generations" (v. 1). In other words, God is and always has been faithful and trustworthy, and we will discover true life only by finding the life He offers in Himself, our ultimate dwelling place. In the first eleven verses of his psalm, Moses meditates on the same transience of life that David confessed. He admits that our lives are like grass that sprouts in the morning and is gone that night, putting it in the familiar context that "a thousand years in Your sight are like yesterday when it passes by, or as a watch in the night" (v. 4).

He first paints the big picture, but then he makes the reality of passing time very personal: "As for the days of our life, they contain seventy years, or if due to strength, eighty years . . . for soon [our life] is gone and we fly away" (v. 10). To paraphrase a popular modern proverb, "Life is short; then you fly." Seventy or eighty years would have been a long, full life when Moses was writing, and yet in relation to eternity it is a "watch in the night." But even though Moses justifiably laments the brevity of life with these words, don't miss that he's also building his case for why we need to take life seriously.

Moses' meditation on the fleeting nature of life leads naturally, yet perhaps a bit surprisingly, into his life-affirming request of God: "Teach us to number our days, that we may present to You a heart of wisdom" (v. 12). Like David, Moses is declaring by way of his prayer the importance of knowing the end from the beginning, of embarking on the journey of life with the destination in mind. The Hebrew word for "to number" can also mean "to prepare," so Moses might also be saying "teach us to prepare our days." Or, to put the request in plain language, "Show us how to plan our lives so we can please You, Lord." It's not just about what to do or be; it's also about who to become—a wise child of God.

The important part of Moses' prayer is the reason he says that we should number our days—so that we can present to God, or enter His presence with, a "heart of wisdom" (v. 12). The Hebrew idea of wisdom incorporates more than just knowledge, understanding, or discernment—it involves being skillful in life and using our lives well for God's glory. As Solomon says in the book of Proverbs, his collection of wise sayings, "The wisdom of the sensible is to understand his way" (14:8), or what could be understood more specifically as "his life." God wants us to be sensible about our lives and to make the most of all the days He gives us.

As a divine parent, God the Father is a model for our parenting. What God wants for us, His children, is simply to live well—to use all the days He gives us to please Him. And not coincidentally, that's also what we naturally desire for our own children—for them to enjoy their lives and live fully for God. That's why we need to number their days. We want to make sure we prepare our children to live wisely and well and for God's glory. A full and meaningful life will not happen by chance but by thoughtful planning and a heart turned to follow God.

❧ ❧

So as our family grew—with Sarah born in 1984, Joel in 1986, Nathan in 1989, and Joy in 1995—we increasingly made numbering our children's days a priority of our parenting. We still tried to have our weekly planning breakfasts, but overseas ministry, numerous moves, and then living out in the country forced us to be more creative about planning. Whenever and however it happened, though, we tried to plan weekly for the spiritual influence and training of our children's lives. It was a priority in the patterns and practices of our parenting and family life. We also took time out around September or January each year, sometimes as a weekend getaway, to plan for the year ahead—for us and our children.

Our children would take part in the planning too. When they reached an age where they were able to make a list of some kind (I allowed a lot of latitude in list making), we would involve them in setting their own goals. We never wanted our children to become passively dependent on us to number their days for them. Rather, we wanted to model for them how to begin thinking about their own lives and how to follow our example in setting goals for themselves. We deliberately avoided making it an onerous duty and enforcing list completion by certain times; instead, we modeled goal making as a positive and fun thing to do.

Each child approached planning differently. We didn't insist on one right way but simply enjoyed seeing each of them get involved and excited about planning their lives in ways that made sense to them and reflected their own personality preferences. Whatever they did, and however they did it, we would delight in their goals and affirm their efforts. We focused on the children's work, not just the product of their work. Sally and I were still mostly the ones who were numbering our children's days, but we were also teaching them the first steps in acquiring the habits and skills they would use as young adults to develop a "heart of wisdom" through following the guidance of Moses' prayer.

We considered planning for each child's spiritual life and character development—practices and qualities of their relationship and life with God—to be distinct from planning for their schooling and activities. We would help them develop their own personal goals for Bible reading, Scripture memorization, and prayer, and plan times to do them. We would create charts of varying sizes, colors, and complexity, depending on their age, to help them keep track of their consistency and progress. We used a variety of methods to help them be faithful with chores and meeting other character-development goals. When they reached their teens, although we would engage in planning and spiritual life discussions with them, we began to trust them to make their own plans for their days and for growing in wisdom with God. For our family, we saw the process of planning with our children as a relational, dynamic, and organic process, not as just a task or procedure to be accomplished.

Numbering our children's days was the first lifegiving practice we initiated in our home. It brought the life of God into our midst in very practical and practicable ways for our children. As they began to think about their own goals and how they could follow God and grow in wisdom to please Him, they began to think in terms that brought the reality of God, who is "our dwelling place in all generations" (Psalm 90:1), into their own place of dwelling and their own generation. We were training them to think of God not just as an impersonal source of truth to be known or maker of rules to be followed, but also as the living God in whom they would find real life and develop a real relationship.

As a family, we would gather to describe and discuss our goals, desires, and relationships with God. Whatever came out in those family times was wisdom born of God's presence among us. It was a natural part of our life together with God as a family.

The apostle Paul makes this dynamic connection with God clear: "The mind set on the flesh is death, but the mind set on the Spirit is life and peace" (Romans 8:6). As we engaged with God through His Spirit living in and through us, we were bringing His life into our home. Paul goes on to say, "If Christ is in you, though the body is dead because of sin, yet the spirit is alive because of righteousness" (v. 10). Perhaps the King James Bible gets closer to the literal sense of the words: "The Spirit is life because of righteousness." The Spirit of God who "is life" brings life to our spirits. That is the goal of lifegiving parenting—to bring God's life to our children's lives in our home.

❧ ❧

By now you may be wondering what the first lifegiving heartbeat of "numbering your child's days" means practically, what it looks like in a family. While I've given a few examples in the preceding pages, I don't have the space in this book to describe all the specific things we would do and say, the kinds of goals we would set, and the plans we would make for our lives. For this first heartbeat, though, I think it is important to describe how we set a tone and tempo in our home that allowed numbering our children's days to become part of our natural life rhythms—like a song we would sing just out of the sheer joy of singing it. Your family rhythms and practices may be different, but you can find your own way to purposely practice and cultivate a lifestyle of numbering your—and your child's—days. Following are some practical suggestions for practicing and cultivating the habit of life planning.

Make Habit a Commitment

As long as we're quoting ancient writers, let's throw in a statement by Greek philosopher Aristotle about habit: "Excellence is an art won by training and habituation. . . . We are what we repeatedly do. Excellence, then, is not an act but a habit." In other words, if you become excellent at numbering your child's days, it will be because you've intentionally trained yourself in the habit. It takes will and work to make a habit of pursuing excellence, but the results are worth it.

We had to work hard at creating the habit of planning for us and our children. The planning breakfasts Sally and I enjoyed early in our marriage required very little work to sustain, but as children came along, and as our lives became more complicated by moves and ministry, we had to make ourselves set aside time for our family planning. Fortunately, children tend to like structure and expectations, so as planning became a regular part of our family experience, even our children would occasionally remind us when we needed to make time for it.

There is no foolproof strategy for getting in the habit of numbering your children's days, but here are three simple suggestions that might help. First, enter the planning time on a printed or digital calendar, or create a smartphone reminder. You may have good intentions, but the planning time won't become a firm commitment until you write it down—in ink, in toner, or digitally—somewhere that you'll see. Second, share the date and time with everyone in the family. Asking your children to help keep you accountable will make them feel included and necessary. Third, use a paper or digital planner, or create a written agenda or form that you will use each time you do planning. Familiarity feeds habit, and a formal and shareable account of the planning time, regardless of the method you use, will help keep everyone on the same page.

Keep It All Enjoyable

Plan a planning party! Think of ways to make the family planning time special. Sally was particularly gifted at this and was driven to transform what could be just a family meeting into an enjoyable family event. Even if the time would be short (although our family meetings rarely were brief in our very verbal and engaged family) or she had only a short time to prepare, Sally would regularly make the planning time inviting, fun, and delightful for our children. Every family will have its own idea of what constitutes an enjoyable planning party, but here are a few ideas.

Choose a good meeting place. Whether it's always the same place or always a new place, choose a setting that will be familiar or fun. It can be inside, outside, or some special nonhome location (such as a park, favorite restaurant, or local attraction), but everyone should feel "at home" in some way. When we weren't around our dining room table or on the couches by our fireplace, we might find a shady spot outside or go to a nature center we all enjoyed.

Make your planning space inviting and comfortable. This is easier to do in a home setting than outside or somewhere else, but wherever you are, if it's too hot or too cold, too dirty or too crowded, you and your children can't sit comfortably, or whatever else might make a place uninviting or uncomfortable, you probably won't get much planning done. At home, comfortable chairs and slouchy couches, pillows and blankets, and favorite stuffed animals will create a space your children will want to be in. If you're out, think of whatever you'll need to create a space that will say to your kids, "This will be fun!"

Finally, and very importantly, provide good snacks and beverages. Yes, it is bait, and there's nothing wrong with that. God made His creation for us to enjoy, so you're just cooperating with His design for your children. Some of our favorite baits included hot chocolate and cookies by the fire, a cold drink and piece of cake outside, hot tea and buttery cinnamon toast on the deck, and . . . You get the idea. If it was a treat the children didn't normally get during the week, it would be all the more inviting. If you feed them, they will come. And treats will keep everyone in a good mood for the time together.

Focus on the Positives

Let's be honest. Talking about goals and plans sounds innocent enough, but it can easily slide into the "dark side" of planning—dealing with unrealistic expectations, performance pressure, guilt, laziness, and more. There is a time and place to talk with your kids (or yourself!) about failed plans and missed goals, but your family planning is not that time or place. Make a special effort to keep this time positive and forward looking, not critical and backward looking. That will at times be difficult, especially when it comes to your children's personal goals about household duties or daily routines, but resist the parental need to confront and correct and focus instead on your parental privilege to encourage and direct. Here are a few thoughts for staying positive.

Ask questions. Don't ask closed-ended questions answerable only with a yes, no, or I don't know; ask open-ended ones that invite your children to share an opinion, insight, or evaluation. Verbal interaction will be the lifeblood of a good planning time, so keep it flowing. Even if you have some concerns, negative questions (Why didn't you . . . ? How did that happen? When did you think . . . ?) will shut down hearts and conversations; positive ones (What do you want to try? What did you learn? How can I help?) will keep hearts and mouths open.

Keep it light. Your children love to laugh, and they love to laugh together with you. Always look for the humor in your lives (it's there), tell some jokes (even if you have to look some up beforehand), and tease and be playful with your kids and your spouse. Whether your children are young or already in their teens, when you keep your planning time light and fun, they will feel safe to let down their guards and be a part of this special family time. As a dad with a more introverted and analytical personality, I had to train myself to be positive and fun. If I learned to lighten up, then anyone can.

Practice grace. We tend to think that giving others grace is just overlooking their sins or errors, like giving them a "Get Out of Jail Free" card when they break God's law. But God's grace doesn't work that way—it doesn't overlook sin but offers love and mercy rather than condemnation and guilt. When we offer grace to children, we're not excusing their sins or failures but are simply affirming our love and belief in them and in what God is doing in their lives. Like many things in the Christian life, practicing grace can seem at odds with our natural parental urges to correct, but it is simply offering what Jesus came to give us: "Of His fullness we have all received, and grace upon grace. For the Law was given through Moses; grace and truth were realized through Jesus Christ" (John 1:16-17). No matter how careful their plans and how doable their goals may be, our children will occasionally fall short of their good intentions. That's when we can offer understanding (since we've been there) and help and express our belief in them. "Focusing on the positives" might sound a bit trite and shallow, but in reality it can also be an exercise of practicing God's grace. And that will go deep into your children's hearts.

❧ ☙

Numbering your child's days may not sound on the surface like a biblical priority of parenting, but think about parenting as though you were Commander Jim Lovell on the ill-fated flight of *Apollo 13*. On the return leg of their aborted moon mission, as the astronauts fought to control their crippled flight module, Commander Lovell had to make a manual course correction, relying only on a wristwatch and his own handwritten math, engineering skills, and jet-pilot instincts to steer the craft safely back home.

Fortunately, like the commander, you have the opportunity as a parent to steer the craft of your family safely home. Small choices like a family planning time may seem unimportant to you now, but they could be helping to set the trajectory of your children's lives, sending them on a path to find life in God in your home. My desire is to help you become a lifegiving parent who confidently steers the modules of your children's hearts into the life of God. The simple course correction of beginning to number your children's days—of beginning to parent them with the end in mind—could be the one that points you, and them, safely home on this journey of life with God.

Even though Moses had adults like you and me in mind when he wrote in Psalm 90 about numbering our days, I think it's fair to say, from his words in the Shema prayer discussed in chapter 1, that he would have heartily agreed that parents must choose to number their children's days as well. In fact, I think that will be even more clear in the final chapter when we look at Psalm 78, which refers back to the Shema and admonishes parents to put their children on the right path. If there's one thing that Scripture teaches about parenting, it's that our first order of business is to direct our children on the path of life with God. That is why it is so important that they see the living God alive in our homes.

The apostle Paul also has something to say about the idea that our time on earth is limited, the same kind of insight that David and Moses expressed in their psalms. The passage is tucked away in Paul's letter to the Ephesians in a somewhat lengthy list of exhortations to the churches in Asia Minor. I think it bears directly on the parenting task of numbering our children's days:

> Be very careful, then, how you live—not as unwise but as wise, making the most of every opportunity, because the days are evil. Therefore do not be foolish, but understand what the Lord's will is.
>
> EPHESIANS 5:15-17, NIV

Paul exhorts the readers of his letter to be careful in how they choose to live, or literally "how you are walking." Just as Moses says in Psalm 90 that a heart of wisdom was the goal of our lives, Paul agrees that living wisely should be our goal. He then gives another nod to Moses, saying that the way to live wisely is by "making the most of every opportunity." A more direct wording, as rendered by other translations, is that we live wisely by "redeeming the time." Paul uses this same word for "redeeming" in his letter to the Galatians to express how Christ has redeemed us from slavery under the Law. It comes from a legal term for the price required to purchase a person out of slavery. Finally, the "time" that is being redeemed is not just the chronological passing of time that governs our days (*chronos*), but the fixed season or measured portion of time in which we're living (*kairos*). For yourself as a parent, think in terms of your season of parenting.

This rich verse can apply both to your time and to your child's time. When you redeem the set time you're given for your season of parenting, you're purchasing it out of slavery to the world and setting it free for God's use. The price of that purchase is your decision to number your days to present to God a heart of wisdom. In the same way, when you number your child's days, you're purchasing their time—their season of childhood—out of slavery to the world and setting it free for seeking God and His wisdom. You are redeeming time so you can stop being slaves to the world and instead become servants of Christ, the One who redeems. Paul ends his exhortation with an extra reminder to choose the path of wisdom because it is the will of God.

∾ ∾

Numbering your children's days is less about accomplishing yet one more task of parenting and more about creating a rhythm of life in your family. Think of it in the same vein as the feasts of Israel, or the seasons of the church year. Both are ways to mark the passing of time in our lives, but they are much more than that—they help us to number the transient days we have on this earth in order to wisely redeem our time for God's use. In liturgical traditions, the church year calendar helps us come to each season, such as Lent or Advent, with a spiritual purpose and intent. We don't live out our days randomly and meaninglessly, but in an ordered way that imbues every season with meaning from God's life and the life, death, and resurrection of Jesus, our Savior. We aren't just marking off minutes and hours of *chronos* time until we "fly away" into eternity; we're making the most of every season of *kairos* time we have until we meet God in a new season of eternal time.

All of these seasons, habits, and traditions of life will bring meaning to your family, just as they do to the church. Every church, even if it's not from a liturgical tradition, contains some form of liturgy—the rhythms and rituals that shape its identity. In the same way, I also believe that every family has a liturgy of some kind, a combination of rhythms and rituals that defines who they are and what's important to them. In a sense, the work you do as a family is to live into the *kairos* time you are given. The Greek word for "liturgy" (*leitourgia*) literally means the "work of the people." It's what we do as people of a church, or of a family, that defines and directs who we are.

Sally and Sarah's book, *The Lifegiving Home*, and Sally's book *The Lifegiving Table* explore the habits, rhythms, and traditions we practiced in the Clarkson home that helped us live into the seasons of our lives with meaning and purpose and defined our identity as a family who walks and works with God. These traditions were unquestionably a part of numbering our children's days, and perhaps even the most important part—the culture of life with God in which they would learn to plan their lives. Without the family devotions, bedtime rituals, Advent rhythms, Christmas habits, Easter readings, table traditions, birthday and holiday meals, and so much more, our planning habits would have been much less meaningful. Numbering our children's days made sense only because Sally and I were numbering our own days.

So start now. Become a lifegiving parent who is numbering your children's days to ensure they are on the path to life in God. As David tells God, "You will make known to me the path of life" (Psalm 16:11). You can make the source of that life known in your home. It starts with numbering your days so that you may present to the living God a heart of wisdom.

Sally's Lifegiving Momoirs

Even as a young girl, Joy held herself to high standards and was very goal oriented. She told me once that when she was ten

NUMBERING YOUR CHILD'S DAYS   ✳   37

years old, she wrote a special entry in her journal about what she
wanted to become when she was a teenager. She wrote down,
"My ten-year-old self wants me to be . . ." and then listed all the
character qualities and other goals she envisioned for herself when
she reached her teens—including being a good daughter, a hard
worker, a faithful friend, morally pure, and a good Christian. When
she was fourteen, she went back and read what she had written.
She told me then, "I hope I'm becoming all the ideals I said I
wanted to become, because it's really hard to keep them all in
mind as a teenager." She even gave a speech on this in a class,
answering the question, Am I becoming the person my ten-year-
old self wanted to be?

Joy is the last and youngest child—there was a six-year gap
between her and Nathan, nine years between her and Joel, and
eleven years between her and Sarah. She was always watching
the older kids and noticing their behavior and choices. At ten, she
would say in her youthful idealism that she would *never* be like
her older teenaged siblings. She would be different. But she told
me that when she became a teenager, she discovered that her ten-
year-old self had held her to some very high standards. It was not
as easy as she thought being the teenager she once envisioned she
would become. Even so, she told me how thankful she was for the
spiritual training and habits she had developed at home during
childhood and how they helped her stay faithful to God as a young
teen. It was a delight to watch her growing into a strong young
woman of God.

Joy has always been a planner, dreamer, and leader. When something needed doing in a group, she would take the lead. It was just in
her nature. She has always been forward minded, and she has a plan
in mind for whatever is ahead. Without question, she is the child
who really took to numbering her days. She had the big picture of
life in mind, and it shaped her dreams, plans, and choices. She was

always making plans for family, ministry, friendships, activities, and projects. Perhaps she inherited some of Clay's list-making genes, or perhaps it was just her natural idealism and vision that moved her forward. Whatever it was, things would get done when they were on Joy's radar. Now that she's already earned a master's degree and has begun her doctorate at such a young age, I look back and see the habits and patterns in her life that enabled her to achieve so much so soon. Like that ten-year-old Joy, she is still looking ahead, making goals, and wondering what she'll become.

Lifegiving ParenTips

Start with your own heart. Number your children's days not just for what you need to help them become but also for what you need to become for them. The four-to-fourteen window for your children's hearts is fully open only briefly, so you need to get your own heart right with God in order to influence your children's hearts for God. They already have a childlike expectation that you will provide for them and direct them—it is present in every child by God's design. That means you need to invest some time thinking about both what they will need from you and what you want them to receive from you—and then setting about to become that person. Plan a time to get away alone to hear from God. What habits, appetites, rhythms, character qualities, and other issues in your life will you need to work on? How are you feeding your own spirit and soul so you can feed your children's? What topical Bible studies do you need to do for yourself that you'll want to share with your children?

Set kid-sized goals. Training your children how to set goals, even at a young age, is giving them early practice at one aspect of what it means to be a disciple of Christ. In Luke 14:26-33, Jesus describes the qualities of those who would make successful disciples. His illustrations of a person building a tower and of a king going out to battle include the principles of counting the cost and making sacrifices for worthy goals. Those principles can be encouraged early on by helping your children create goals that will require some actual cost and sacrifice, such as earning money to purchase a desired item, building or making something, learning a skill, or earning a new privilege or reward. You can provide reasonable and attractive incentives to motivate them to pursue their goals. Help them establish dated milestones and create visual charts or posters to gauge their progress. These child-sized goals may seem like small steps of training, but they can become big steps on the path of discipleship.

Use child-friendly tools. When your children are old enough to begin participating more directly in planning for their lives, introduce them to some simple planning tools. They might not use them regularly or completely, but even if it is just for a while, you will be teaching them some principles and practices of planning. For instance, I created what I called "My 'Check Me Out' DependableList" for our children when they were younger. It was a positive check-off list (no writing required) that provided a kid-friendly way to develop a daily habit, even if for just a couple of minutes, of evaluating their attitudes and the accomplishment of chores and responsibilities. As they got older, I designed other planning forms that required more evaluation or gave them their own planning calendar notebooks. Each child will plan differently depending on their personality. The important part of trying out different tools is simply to keep the principles in play so they become habits.

Starting the Heartbeat of Parental Lifegiving

Numbering your child's days starts with the long view that life is short. When you begin parenting with the end in mind, you will make the most of the time you have to shape and influence your child's heart and mind for God.

CHAPTER 3

NURTURING YOUR CHILD'S SPIRIT

*Fathers, do not provoke your children to anger, but bring them
up in the discipline and instruction of the Lord.*

EPHESIANS 6:4

BACK IN THE DAY when our children had only one slow computer
with a single log-in to share, they each understandably made the
most of whatever screen time they were allotted. The three older
children were reasonably proficient with the Windows 95 interface
and their installed educational programs. Occasionally I would be
called in to solve a Windows system problem, but most of the time
the kids were on their own and did just fine.

Until the day I heard boy noises emanating from the sunken den
where the family computer resided. When I went in, I found Joel,
then around nine years old, at the computer, overcome with obvious
little-boy anger and frustration. I surmised he must be upset about
the results of a game or program he was using, and he certainly
needed my gentle intervention about exercising self-control.

I motioned him over to the couch, where he sat down hard with
folded arms and an angry scowl. I engaged in my wise-father role

to settle him down and talk about self-control and patience. I even quoted some good Scriptures. As Joel's countenance and spirit softened, I sent him off to do something else, satisfied with the successful outcome of my dadly wisdom. It wasn't until later that I discovered *I* was the one who needed the intervention and Joel had every right to be frustrated.

It turned out that Joel was never upset by what the computer was actually doing. If the problem had been a misbehaving program or a frustrating game, he would have just quit that one and tried another. Easy enough. Joel wasn't frustrated by what the computer was doing; he was frustrated by what it should have been doing but wasn't. And that's where I come in.

It seems that in my very systematic (some would say obsessive) tendency to want computer files and icons organized logically and efficiently, I had done some tweaking of the kids' Windows desktop the day before. It was not a big deal to me, but it was to Joel. He was rightfully exasperated that the computer was not as it had been and was not doing what it was supposed to do.

Once I had offered Joel my humbling mea culpa, I got to thinking about a parenting verse I had been studying, and it suddenly became clearer. It's a short exhortation to fathers, a single verse tucked into a longer section about household relationships (husbands, wives, children, fathers, servants, masters) in Paul's letter to the Ephesians: "Fathers, do not provoke your children to anger, but bring them up in the discipline and instruction of the Lord" (Ephesians 6:4).

❧ ❦

Paul's exhortation is not just well-meaning apostolic advice or a strong suggestion to Christian dads, which is also just as applicable for Christian moms; it's an imperative. The force of Paul's command is closer to "Fathers, stop provoking your children to anger!" He uses similar language in a letter to the Colossian church written around the same time: "Fathers, do not exasperate your children, so that they will not lose heart" (3:21). In other words, don't stir up your children to anger to the point that they become dispirited and you lose the ability to reach their hearts. Your child's spirit, or heart, is the inner person who, despite sin, is stamped with God's image and drawn to you, the parent, by divine design. If you lose your children's hearts, you also disrupt their relationships with God.

After the first negative command in Ephesians 6:4 for fathers to stop what they were doing, Paul offers a second, positive command for fathers to start doing something else: "But bring them up!" The conjunction ("but") in this context could be rendered "instead" or "rather," contrasting the second command with the first one. So instead of provoking their children to anger, fathers are to "bring them up." To our ears today, those words suggest child raising in general—being good Christian parents who raise their children to be good Christians. But there's more to it.

What Paul is really saying is this: "Instead, nurture them!" When you hear the word *nurture*, you probably think of a mother with her children, or even of a mother nursing an infant at her breast. It's a very lifegiving kind of word and probably not a parenting term you would typically associate with fathers. But Paul does. The New Testament uses three words for "nurture"; the one here is used only twice—both times in Ephesians, and both times in reference to men.

The Greek term Paul uses, *ektrepho*, means literally "to feed from." It certainly sounds like a motherly term. However, the only other time Paul uses it is just eight verses earlier, where he writes, "In this same way, husbands ought to love their wives as their own bodies. He who loves his wife loves himself. After all, no one ever hated his own body, but he *feeds* and cares for it, just as Christ does the church" (5:28-29, NIV; emphasis added). According to Paul, a husband expresses godly love for his wife when he "feeds" (nurtures) and cares for her—he treats her as a person who requires special care and attention. A husband does that by feeding his wife's spirit from his own, and since they are one in Christ, he is actually nourishing the life they share in Him.

Eight verses later (6:4), Paul uses the same word to exhort the fathers in his audience to nurture (bring up) their children. This time it's the children (*tekna*, children of indeterminate age) who need the "feeding from," and it's the fathers' responsibility to feed them. Paul instructs them how to nurture their children—by "the discipline and instruction of the Lord." These two closely related terms, *discipline* and *instruction*, are relational words that focus on training and admonishing. The way the text is written suggests that the two words can be considered as a single act of influence that is to be done "of the Lord." However, we'll look at each word individually later.

Paul's "of the Lord" is arguably a deliberate challenge of the Roman concept of *patria potestas*, or "power of a father," that the Ephesian fathers would have known and practiced by default— the absolute, unquestioned power of a father over his children. In contrast, Paul implies, believing fathers were to nurture their children by the discipline and instruction that is "of the Lord"—feeding their sons and daughters from the same Spirit of Christ who was now in their lives. The ownership of their children was no longer theirs but the Lord's, a significant change for those fathers as new Christians.

So what do all the details of this passage have to do with my parental misfire regarding frustrated Joel and the errant computer? As I pondered what happened with Joel, I began to understand better what Paul was saying—that children, designed by God to expect parents to nurture them, become frustrated when that nurture doesn't happen. In other words, it wasn't only what the children of these Ephesian families were receiving that left them exasperated but also—and possibly more importantly—what they should have been receiving but were *not*: the training and instruction in the Lord that God had designed their spirits to expect. They were not being nurtured.

Nurture is the very essence of the lifegiving parenting this book is about—giving God's life to our children, feeding their spirits with the life of Christ from our own spirits. It's not just warm hugs, sweet words, and good feels—it is discipline and instruction, training and admonition. Nurture is hands-on and hands-around parenting. It cannot be done with a book, video, or new app. It doesn't happen by sending our children to Sunday school, Bible club, or camp. We cannot delegate nurture to another person or program. Only we as parents can nurture our children. That's why Paul makes it a command, not a suggestion or an option—it's a matter of obedience, not preference.

⁓ ⁓

There are many ways to talk about what nurture should look like in your home. When Sally and I were in our early days of parenting, we started talking about how to give our children the gifts of life in Christ. The idea of "life gifts" soon led to an acrostic of the word "GIFTS," which would become the nurturing model we would use for our family for many years of "bringing up" our children. The nurturing LifeGIFTS we gave them were Grace, Inspiration, Faith, Training, and Service.

There are many such models you can use, but arguably the most natural model for biblical nurture as part of lifegiving parenting is the one Paul recommended—the discipline and instruction of the Lord. But what does it mean practically to discipline and instruct your children, and for those nurturing activities to be "of the Lord"? What will they look like lived out in your Christian home? There are three ways that Paul tells the Ephesian fathers nurture can be expressed—by training, by instruction, and by modeling.

Nurturing by Training ("Discipline")

While the word *discipline* is sometimes applied to adults in Scripture, it's probably safe to say that when you hear the word, you think first of parental correction or punishment of a child. Both ideas are certainly part of biblical discipline that you will exercise as a parent, but there is much more to the concept.

Discipline of children in the Bible is a two-sided coin. On the one side, it is negative and backward looking—it is the correction a parent applies when children stray from God's path that brings them back to the path. On the other side, it is positive and forward looking—it is the process by which parents lovingly lead their children along God's path to help them learn what it means to please Him. From a New Testament perspective, it is all training—whether negative or positive—for becoming a godly Christian.

The Ephesian fathers reading or hearing Paul's letter would have taken the term *paideia*, translated as "discipline" in Ephesians 6:4, to mean the general training of a child, including through teaching or instruction, as it is often translated. It's also helpful to understand that Paul's words likely would have evoked for the Ephesian fathers the kind of training, or teaching, described in the Shema of Deuteronomy 6:4-9—that of sharpening a child like a knife. Training is more than just behavioral conditioning; it is shaping and forming the heart. Training is an ongoing sharpening process in a child's life of reinforcing the truths of God.

The New Testament talks about the experience of training in a variety of ways. Training might be hard or painful, as described in Hebrews 12:7-11—a rigorous guide to creating holiness. Training from the actual words of Scripture can direct a person toward righteousness —2 Timothy 3:16. It can teach us "to say 'No' to ungodliness and worldly passions, and to live self-controlled, upright and godly lives" as described in Titus 2:11-13 (NIV). Whatever form it takes, parents who nurture by training are influencing their children out of their own adult understanding, experience, and Christian maturity to help them live in a way that will please God. There is nothing strict, harsh, or formal suggested in Paul's words—he's describing training that is personal and relational.

For a lifegiving parent, nurturing by training is all about showing children that the purpose of training is not just to make them behave, or stop behaving, in a certain way, but primarily to help them see God at work in their lives and increase their willingness and ability to please Him. That means you must be involved personally in the training so you can feed your children out of your own life in Christ.

Training our children encompasses all areas of life as we discipline them to respond to different situations in ways that honor God and reflect what He wants for our lives. While training can and does take place as we go through each day, there are a few specific areas that provide the opportunity to train our children in a nurturing, lifegiving way.

Chores and responsibilities. This seems like a no-brainer area of training, but it is all too easy for it to become a no-hearter, too. From the time our children were little, we let them know that doing chores was simply a part of being a family, and they were helping to make our house into a place where Jesus would feel at home. Whenever possible, we would make chores a shared family experience, not just jobs to complete. Our goal was to engage our children's hearts and help them understand that God was part of our "home work" as well as every other part of our lives.

Family values. We've always held that family values are best caught when taught, which is why we purposely trained our children to know and appreciate ours. I created a list called "Our 24 Family Ways" that provided four biblically based statements of values in each of six areas of family life: authorities, relationships, possessions, work, attitudes, and choices. They reflected the heart of God in everything we did at home. We made memorizing and discussing the Ways together a regular part of our nurture and training. (See chapter 7 for more discussion of this.)

Hospitality. There may be no better way to bring the life of God into your home than by practicing biblical hospitality. Jesus said that showing hospitality to "the least of these" (those who are hungry, thirsty, strangers, naked, sick, prisoners) was to show it directly to Him (see Matthew 25:34-40). We trained our children to be hospitable hosts whenever we had guests in our home—greeting, speaking, serving, listening. We wanted them to know that in addition to serving Jesus, they might also be "entertain[ing] angels without knowing it" (Hebrews 13:2). It was a tangible way for them to see the Spirit of God alive in our home.

Nurturing by Instruction

Because we tend to think of instruction as didactic exercises aimed at children's minds, we can easily miss the relational aspect of it as an act of nurturing their spirits. The term Paul uses in Ephesians 6:4, *nouthesia,* is used only three times in the New Testament, and only in the Ephesians passage is it applied to children. Literally, the term means to "put in the mind," but it is often translated as "admonish," with the idea of offering a warning. Paul is suggesting instruction that is not just a process of providing *information* but is also a means of encouraging *transformation.* It's about nurturing the spirit, not just filling the mind.

Jesus said, "A pupil [a disciple, or learner] is not above his teacher; but everyone, after he has been fully trained [made adequate, or qualified], will be like his teacher" (Luke 6:40). Clearly Jesus, the greatest of all teachers, understood that instruction was about changing lives and creating disciples. Dr. Lawrence Richards, an authority on Christian education and Bible teaching, affirms the idea behind both Jesus' words and Paul's exhortation: "The teaching that Scripture finds significant is not that which provides information alone but also the teaching that creates disciples who live in responsive obedience to God's will."[1]

It raises a natural question: What makes the difference between instruction that fills the mind and instruction that fuels the heart? As parents, how can we instruct our children in a way that reaches their hearts and nurtures their spirits? What will make our instruction lifegiving? Part of the answer begins with understanding the dynamics of the information age in which we and our children live.

We're all exposed to cultural sources of information and influence, absorbing much of their content passively or by default. Radio, television, magazines, digital music, mobile apps, websites, streaming video—these all by their natures consume increasing portions of the time that families would otherwise spend talking, reading, and engaging verbally with one another. For all the advantages we've gained through media, we've lost the natural, undistracted interconnectedness that once characterized families. To overcome that loss, parents have to work harder and smarter to make the kinds of nurturing, lifegiving connections for instruction that Paul suggests.

Jesus taught the deepest, truest, and most profound ideas ever spoken. The apostle John writes, "In the beginning was the Word, and the Word was with God, and the Word was God. . . . And the Word became flesh, and dwelt among us, and we saw His glory, glory as of the only begotten from the Father, full of grace and truth" (John 1:1, 14). If Jesus, the eternal Word of God, full of grace and truth, is in us by His Spirit, then we can offer those qualities to our children. However, it is also possible we can get the truth right in our instruction but miss the grace. Jesus' instruction contained not only propositional truths but also truths conveyed through parables, stories, anecdotes, analogies, illustrations from nature, physical touch, and tone of voice—not to mention through miracles, healings, and supernatural events. Perhaps it's in that kind of interactional instruction that grace can find expression too.

If we're not instructing our children the way Jesus teaches us to, we're neglecting a part of nurturing their spirits. When we let that part of Christ that lives in us be seen by our children through our gracious instruction, they'll get a small glimpse of the life of God. In our home, instructing with grace meant telling stories about brave children who had faith in the face of fear, or sharing parables about familiar people and places to illustrate a truth about God's Kingdom, or using nature to create an analogy about God's blessings and faithfulness. It also meant looking in our children's eyes, touching them tenderly to make a point, reading Scripture with feeling and expression, and talking with them about God as we walked along the way. That kind of instruction brought the life of Christ into our home. Following are some approaches that can help you instruct your children in a nurturing, lifegiving way.

Illustrations. What do you remember most from your pastor's sermons? There are many words, facts, details, and outline points you'll forget, but you'll likely remember a thoughtful illustration. Why is that? Because an illustration engages the imagination—it gives an idea or an abstract truth a way to be understood concretely. You can explain to your children about God's forgiveness through Jesus' payment for our sin and get a nodding head. But tell them about a judge who must declare his own son guilty but then comes off the bench to pay the penalty himself, and you'll see the light of understanding turn on in their eyes. A thoughtful illustration puts the flesh of imagination on the bones of truth.

Stories. Illustrations and anecdotes tend to be short and to the point. Stories take more time to tell well, yet they will capture your children's imaginations and take them on a journey. The power of story for lifegiving instruction is that a good one creates memorable pictures in your children's minds that become anchors of meaning. That's why Jesus' parables were so powerful—the Prodigal Son, the Good Samaritan, the Sower, the Good Steward. These names alone likely evoke the character, actions, and feelings associated with each one. Use stories whenever you can with your children to instruct them in general truths about the Christian life. You'll be surprised one day when they're grown to hear them share about a story you told and what they learned from it.

Bible topics. One of the common instructional experiences in our home was topical Bible studies. If someone had a question about a matter of faith, something came up in the news, or there was interest in what God thought about an issue, we'd get out a concordance and start looking up verses together. When the kids were younger, the studies were faster with fewer Scriptures; as they got older, the studies were longer and more in depth. In either case, we typically talked together about what we had learned, which helped them internalize the lesson or truth. Rather than just an impersonal instructional assignment, topical studies were opportunities for lifegiving instructional nurture.

Nurturing by Modeling ("of the Lord")

It should, but perhaps doesn't, go without saying that training and instruction are ineffective without positive modeling. A portion of Moses' words to the Israelites just before they entered the Promised Land brought together the three qualities of nurturing children's spirits in one exhortation for parents—they were to teach their children diligently (instruction), reinforce that truth continuously (training), and express the truth that they would love the Lord completely and faithfully in their lives and homes (modeling) (Deuteronomy 6:4-9; see chapter 1). Paul, fifteen hundred years later, reminded the Ephesian fathers of that same principle—that their training and instruction was to be "of the Lord." God's life was to be modeled in their lives.

When Jesus began to gather His disciples, it was clear that His purpose was to teach and train by becoming a model for them. In his Gospel, Mark recalled that Jesus "appointed twelve, so that they would be with Him" (3:14). They were together—with Him—for three years to prepare them to be God's instruments in starting the church after Jesus' death, resurrection, and ascension. The very last thing Jesus said to His disciples, after commissioning them to go into the world and make disciples, was that He would be with them: "I am with you always, even to the end of the age" (Matthew 28:20).

Paul himself also lived by this principle of modeling: "Be imitators of me, just as I also am of Christ" (1 Corinthians 11:1); "The things you have learned and received and heard and seen in me, practice these things, and the God of peace will be with you" (Philippians 4:9); "Therefore as you have received Christ Jesus the Lord, so walk in Him" (Colossians 2:6). And those Ephesian fathers would have already read or heard another of Paul's "with Him" admonitions earlier in his letter: "Be imitators of God, as beloved children; and walk in love, just as Christ also loved you" (Ephesians 5:1-2).

None of us likes to be told to practice what we preach, simply because it puts us on alert not to be hypocritical and inconsistent. It's a good admonition, though, and it is the colloquial expression of a central concept for parenting—that parents must model by their lives whatever they train and teach their children to do. Aside from the hypocrisy angle, there is another less-evident principle in the expression that is not quite so off-putting—it is the corresponding truth that you cannot teach your children what you don't already know. Moses made that clear in the Shema: "These commandments that I give you today *are to be on your hearts*. Impress them on your children" (Deuteronomy 6:6-7, NIV; emphasis added). You cannot impress on your children's hearts what is not already on your own.

When Paul tells these Ephesian fathers that their training and instruction is to be "of the Lord," he is suggesting on one level that it should be like the teaching of Jesus and should certainly not be hypocritical and inconsistent. However, he is also saying much more— that it should come from the life of God that is already present in the fathers' hearts through Christ. That modeling and imitation is what will make their training and instruction effective—they will be giving life to their children that they as fathers already possess, impressing on their children's hearts what is already on theirs. That is lifegiving parenting.

While the general principle for both mothers and fathers of modeling for your children what you want them to learn and know may be clear in Scripture, what that will look like is less distinct. Only you will know whether your own life is a model of the kind of Christians you are training and instructing your children to become. Only you will know if your parenting is "of the Lord." Only you will know if you can genuinely encourage your children to imitate your life as you imitate Christ. Only you will know what you need to do to ensure your example is "of the Lord."

Take some time to get away, alone or as a couple, to evaluate how you are modeling authentic Christianity to your children and how you are imitating Christ for them. Look at Galatians 5:22-23 and ask yourselves how your children are seeing the fruit of the Spirit in your lives—"love, joy, peace, patience, kindness, goodness, faithfulness, gentleness, self-control." Ask if your children see you pondering those things that exhibit the qualities listed in Philippians 4:8—whatever is true, honorable, right, pure, lovely, of good repute, excellent, and worthy of praise. Evaluate if they are seeing the "heart" of Colossians 3:12-15 in your hearts—compassion, kindness, humility, gentleness, patience, forbearance, forgiveness, love, unity, peace, and thankfulness.

None of us as parents can live up to all the qualities—all the time—that Paul lists in those passages. He did not intend them to be checklists to determine how far we are from God's ideals, but rather road maps to confirm that we're headed in the right direction. We're all in the process of growing in maturity in Christ, and Paul is simply holding up the ideals so we have a goal to pursue. It's not that we'll reach the goal today, tomorrow, or even in our lifetimes, but that we are consistently moving toward it. And that's exactly what your children need to see—faithfulness in growing in Christ. If you see some qualities in these lists that perhaps are not as strong as you would like in your life, then pray about how to grow in them as a couple. If you're faithful to God, He will be faithful to you and to your children.

We cannot really become lifegiving parents without taking seriously the call to model the life of Christ to our children. It is easy to tell ourselves that if we're training and instructing our children, we're doing what is required of us as parents—we're "bringing them up." But the truly lifegiving part of nurture is in those last three words: "of the Lord." That is where our children will be "fed" by us—from the life of Christ that is already in our spirits.

The concept of parental nurture is not just an accidental idea that Paul threw into his series of exhortations about household rules in his letter to the Ephesians. Remember, the word for "nurture" is first used there in reference to a husband's responsibility for his wife, in a section steeped in theological meaning about Christ and His church. It is not an accident that Paul uses the same term just a few verses later to talk about parental nurture of children, and it is completely reasonable to assume that some of the same depth of theological meaning carries over into the second instance. Paul does not use words casually.

Another of Paul's passages beautifully illustrates the concept of parental nurture he suggests in Ephesians 6:4. It leaves no doubt that Paul recognized the power of nurture in the lives of Jesus' disciples and just as much in families. Paul's words to the church at Thessalonica are a powerful description of nurturing, lifegiving parenting:

> We proved to be gentle among you, *as a nursing mother tenderly cares for her own children*. Having so fond an

affection for you, we were well-pleased to impart to you not only the gospel of God but also *our own lives*, because you had become very dear to us. . . . You are witnesses, and so is God, how devoutly and uprightly and blamelessly we behaved toward you believers; just as you know how we were *exhorting and encouraging and imploring each one of you as a father would his own children*, so that you would *walk in a manner worthy of the God* who calls you into His own kingdom and glory.

I THESSALONIANS 2:7-12, EMPHASIS ADDED

Paul uses unusually warm and personal language to convince the Thessalonian believers of his concern for them. He describes how he was gentle with them, in the same way that a nursing mother would care for her own children, and how he had a longing desire for them. The picture of a nursing mother is a beautiful parallel to the spirit of nurture expressed in the Ephesians verses to husbands and fathers. The fact that Paul mentions not just a mother but a nursing mother suggests that he nurtured the Thessalonian disciples as an act of feeding them from his own life. It is a picture of lifegiving nurture.

Paul goes on to remind the Thessalonians of his devout, upright, and blameless behavior toward them, and then he likens his brief time with them to the actions of a father who exhorts, encourages, and implores his children to walk, or live, in a manner worthy of God. The language he uses is, again, a parallel to the "discipline and instruction" language of the Ephesians passage. It is a picture of an "of the Lord" father (not a *patria potestas* one) whose overriding desire for his own children is that they walk in a way that pleases God. The illustration of the engaged father, just like that of the nursing mother, is a picture of lifegiving nurture.

One last thing worth noting: Don't miss the big picture when Paul says, "We were well-pleased to *impart to you* not only the gospel of God but also *our own lives.*" He is describing the same heartfelt "of the Lord" nurture to which he called the Ephesian fathers—he imparted to them his life, the life of God that was already in him. This is a beautiful biblical description of not only nurturing the spirit of his "children" but also of lifegiving parenting. If you can catch the spirit of what Paul is saying to the Ephesian fathers and the Thessalonian believers, you will be well on your way to becoming a lifegiving parent.

⁂

Nurture can be a little bit of a loaded word for Christians and especially for dads, which may be why translations tend not to use it for *ektrepho.* When it comes to raising children, nurture likely initially sounds to most men's ears like a maternal, not paternal, act of parenting. Fair enough. However, Paul's nurture in Ephesians is not about nursing children or soothing fears after a nightmare but is simply about how parents, and perhaps especially fathers, feed their children with God's training and instruction so they'll grow to be healthy and thriving followers of Christ. Paul's nurture is a lifegiving concept for all parents.

Perhaps an illustration from nature would be helpful in closing to get a different picture of nurture. When I first understood the term *ektrepho* as a compound word meaning to "feed from," the first image that popped into my mind was a bird feeding a chick in the nest. In many cases, a mother bird regurgitates food and feeds it to her nestlings. As it turns out, only about one percent of males feed chicks alone, and only eight percent of females. In the vast majority of bird species, the feeding process is biparental—both the male and female are involved in feeding the chicks. Both mom and dad "feed from" their nestlings together, providing nourishment through their own lifegiving efforts.

Even though Paul addressed fathers in his Ephesians comments, looking at his comments in Thessalonians suggests that he knows that the spiritual nurture of children is a biparental responsibility—both Mom and Dad are needed in the process. You and your spouse are lifegiving parents together, bringing your children into engagement with the life of God in your home by nurturing their spirits. You both are feeding them from the life of God that is in your own spirits, and this is the life that will lead to their own relationships with God as they grow strong and healthy in Him. That's what lifegiving parents do.

Sally's Lifegiving Momoirs

Nurturing my children was not always a planned part of my normal day, but sometimes the spontaneous times of training and instruction were the best times. When we were living in my mother-in-law's small home in the Texas countryside, with the ministry office right next door, I was not able to have much time alone. One morning I got up very early to take a predawn walk just by myself. I tiptoed quietly to the front door, but before I could make my escape, eight-year-old Joel came down the stairs, saw me, and asked if he could go with me. For a moment I thought, *No, this is my time to be alone*, but of course my nurturing mama heart said, "Sure, sweetie." He put on shoes and a jacket, and we quietly left together. He held my hand as we made our way into the morning quiet and darkness and said, "I just love being with you, Mommy."

As we were talking and walking along the country road in the just-breaking dawn, the morning star was still visible in the sky. Joel noted how bright and beautiful it was, so I said, "Did you know that Jesus calls Himself the 'bright morning star'? That's what Jesus wants to be in your heart. As you walk along the path of your life, He wants to be the One that you see and walk toward. He wants to be the brightest star in the sky of your life." Joel was an innocent, loving, and relational child, so he would take things like this into his heart very seriously.

We talked a bit about it, and it was a nice moment—but soon we were back home, and life went on. All these years later, however, he still remembers that story of our early morning walk and tells it when he speaks at conferences. He says that even though it was just one of many such walks I would take, with and without children, it is one he remembers because I took the time to make it special with him. And he still thinks about that image of Jesus as the "bright morning star" in his life now as an adult. This was just one moment of choosing to nurture one of my children—to feed Joel with God's life from my own heart— but that spontaneous object lesson from nature found a place in Joel's heart and mind that probably will be there for the rest of his life.

Lifegiving ParenTips

Learn the language. When you're nurturing your children in the training and instruction of the Lord, you'll need to learn a certain language. If it's new to you, give yourself some time to learn and practice it. The first level of nurturing language is learning how to talk about your faith and the Bible with your children. Part of that is simply learning to be comfortable with spiritual talk; another part is learning to speak in a way that your children will understand; and a final part is learning to take initiative to talk about spiritual things, what you're learning in devotions, and Bible insights. A second level of language is learning how to ask good questions that will be intriguing to your children and will open discussions about spiritual topics. A side issue for language (a challenge for many dads) is learning how to be expressive, excited, and passionate when talking about spiritual matters or Scripture with your children. If you're engaged, they'll be engaged. This can also be true of family prayer.

Trust the organics. It is important to understand this principle for nurturing the spirit: Good things grow in good soil. If you create good soil in your home—you're loving, caring, engaged, teaching, and so on—then you can trust that good soil to grow good hearts in your children. Don't get overly concerned about whether your training and instruction are good enough, or if you're doing enough of one or the other, or if you're doing a good job with the "of the Lord" stuff. If you're anxious and fearful about getting the words and concepts right before you ever begin training and instructing, you might be missing the point. Think more about cultivating a home life that is rich and relational in the things of God and the life of God. Then relax and enjoy your marriage, children, and home. Cultivate the soil of a great Christian home and good things will grow there, including your kids' hearts.

Feed your heart. If nurture is the act of feeding your children from your own life and spirit, then there is an obvious principle that can't be neglected—you must feed your own spirit to have something to feed your children's spirits. You cannot be a source of the Spirit's lifegiving water for your children if the well of your own spirit is empty or dry. Make sure your well stays filled so you'll have living water to give your children. Again, you don't need to become a theologian or spiritual saint of some kind. You only need to be you, living in connection with God. Here are three simple ways to keep your spirit fed and watered for your children. First, set aside a place and time each day to read the Word of God and pray. Second, read interesting Christian books or biographies to feed your spirit. And third, listen regularly to teachers and other Christian speakers you find spiritually and intellectually stimulating. When you are fed, you will have spiritual nourishment to feed to your children.

Starting the Heartbeat of Parental Lifegiving

Nurturing your child's spirit starts with the need to "feed" your child. Godly training, instruction, and modeling become sources of sustenance as you discover that biblical nurture is nourishing your child with the life of God from your own life.

CHAPTER 4

GUARDING YOUR CHILD'S HEART

Guard your heart above all else, for it determines the course of your life.

PROVERBS 4:23, NLT

FOR SEVERAL YEARS when our children were younger, we had a friend living in our home. David, a ten-year-old boy, was so delightful that we would spend hours on the couch sipping hot chocolate and listening to his stories with rapt attention. We set aside days for just David, when we would celebrate his music (he was a violinist), enter into his world, and enjoy his company. When we told our friends about David, they would invite him to come live in their homes too. Oh, I should mention that David was not a real boy; he was a literary character, the namesake of the 1916 novel *Just David*. Even so, our young friend in print was like a member of our household—and a wonderful example of a guarded heart.

Just David was written by Eleanor H. Porter, who had become a bestselling author with her more familiar novel, *Pollyanna*, three years earlier. Porter was a devoted optimist, like her alter ego, Pollyanna, known to many as the "Glad Girl." Despite the oppressive weight of World War I, her signature idealism found a new expression in David. In him she presents a literary apologetic for both the ideal of a protected childhood that allows a child to grow up strong in mind and spirit, unadulterated by the adult world, and the ideal of cultivating in a child mental and spiritual appetites for what is beautiful, good, and true in life.

Our children were about fifteen, twelve, ten, and four when we first met David. We were only a few years into our growing family ministry of helping parents raise wholehearted Christian children, and we were always on the lookout for new books to recommend. We thought young David was such an appealing literary model of a wholehearted child that we searched out a first-edition copy of the book, put it back into print, and introduced thousands of other families to the story of David.

I mention *Just David* here because his literary life illustrates the concept of guarding a child's heart. The story opens in a secluded mountain cabin where David's father had moved with his son six years before with a very specific purpose in mind. Now David's father knows he is dying and that David will need to go back to the world from which he had removed him. Though ill, he begins to walk David down the mountain path to the village below, wondering if what he has done in those six years will mean anything.

> All this the man had planned carefully. He had meant that only the good and beautiful should have place in David's youth. It was not that he intended that evil, unhappiness, and death should lack definition, only definiteness, in the boy's mind. It should be a case where the good and the beautiful should so fill the thoughts that there would be no room for anything else. This had been his plan.[1]

The rest of the book is about David's new life in the village, with both beauty-deprived and beauty-filled townspeople who take him in after his father's death. It's about how David's guarded heart prepared him for the new life and people he would encounter and how his innocence and goodness brought needed beauty and life to the world he found.

Just David is only a story, a novel written a century ago, and yet it touches on hopes that are perhaps particularly distinctive to Christian parents. As believers, we feel a godly responsibility to protect our children's innocence and guard their hearts. We want our children to value the beauty and goodness of this world God has made for us and not to be changed by the ugliness and evil we know they will encounter. We hope our children will grow up to touch others with the ideals of God's life, beauty, and goodness. We want our children to be like David.

⊰ ⊱

The problem with ideals, though, is that they're just so idealistic. No matter how hard we try to help our children stay on the straight and narrow way, how diligently we try to guard their eye and ear gates, how much we try to model and train them to practice the Golden Rule, they are constantly tempted to be pulled away from God's ideals. Truly faith-driven parents will never completely give up on their biblical standards, and yet the longer we are on the parenting journey, the more we may let go of our tight grip on what we believe Scripture teaches about parenting. But that doesn't change the realness of the ideals.

For more than twenty-five years, Sally and I have made it our mission to champion the biblical ideals of Christian parenting expressed in passages such as Deuteronomy 6:4-9 (see chapter 1) and Ephesians 6:4 (see chapter 3)—ideals such as wholeheartedly teaching our children the truths and wisdom of God, bringing them up in the training and instruction of the Lord, guarding their hearts, and sharing with them the life of God. We hold them up unapologetically as divinely defined goals toward which every parent should be moving. Realistically, we know very few parents will ever claim they have reached the goal, and neither do we. However, the successful parent is not the one who reaches the goal, but the one who faithfully keeps moving toward it. Successful parenting is in the faithful pursuit, not the ultimate goal.

Sally and I often talk about the path of parenting, one marked off by our growth in Christ and faithfulness to God's instructions to parents. We teach that successful parenting is simply figuring out where you should be on that path, stepping onto it, and beginning to move faithfully toward the ideals of godly parenting from there. It doesn't matter where you start—at the beginning, in the middle, or further on—it is your faithful progress that makes you a successful parent.

What I don't want you to miss is why the biblical ideals are necessary. If we have no ultimate goal, then we have no path forward. We are vulnerable to following the latest parenting expert or the newest formula. However, when biblical parenting ideals are our ultimate destination, we have a path to follow by faith—one that we know will be pleasing to God: "Without faith it is impossible to please [God], for he who comes to God must believe that He is and that He is a rewarder of those who seek Him" (Hebrews 11:6).

The principles of lifegiving parenting in this book are some of the points along the path that will keep you moving toward the goal. They are not the only points, and they're not a formula for or promise of success, but they can move you forward by faith toward being the kind of faithful and loving parents that you foresaw when you started your parenting journey. Lifegiving parenting will help you bring the life of God into your home and your children's lives, helping them become the kind of people you envision in your spirit—those who will love what is good and not be corrupted by the evil and ugliness they encounter in the world. Like David's father, a lifegiving parent, you can guard your children's hearts and plan that "the good and the beautiful" will define their lives.

﹪ ﹫

A literary example is inspiring, but what about a biblical example? Solomon was the wisest man of all the east and Egypt during his time, a man with "very great discernment and breadth of mind" (1 Kings 4:29). He was hardly the ideal model for a godly parent, but his wisdom and words as a father shine a light on how we should approach raising children. In the first nine chapters of Proverbs, Solomon admonishes his sons to follow the wisdom and instruction they have learned from him and their mother. In chapter 4 he turns his attention especially to the path of parenting we walk with our children.[2]

Solomon starts out Proverbs 4 recalling his own youth and how his father, King David, had encouraged him to hold fast to his father's words, keep his commandments, and above all acquire wisdom and understanding (see vv. 3-9). David assured his son Solomon, "Do not forsake [wisdom], and she will *guard* you; love her, and she will *watch over* you" (v. 6, emphasis added). Two times in chapter 4, Solomon talks about providing a "guard" for a child's heart (see also 2:7-11 and 3:23-26). He learned the concept from his father and now is passing it on as a father.

Solomon then begins to address his own sons, enjoining them to listen to his instruction and follow "the way of wisdom." He assures them that choosing to walk on that path will be a guard of protection for them, but that they also need to guard the instruction they have received: "I have directed you in the way of wisdom; I have led you in upright paths. When you walk, your steps will not be impeded;

and if you run, you will not stumble. Take hold of instruction; do not let go. Guard her, for she is your life" (vv. 10-13).

After warning them to avoid "the path of the wicked and . . . the way of evil men" (v. 14), Solomon conveys one of the most evocative depictions of the path of parenting recorded in Scripture, a picture of the task we face from the very beginnings of our journeys. It shines like a hidden jewel of truth in the fields of parental wisdom: "The path of the righteous is like the light of dawn, that shines brighter and brighter until the full day. The way of the wicked is like darkness; they do not know over what they stumble" (vv. 18-19).

Solomon tells his sons in a picture what he has discovered and done as a parent. He has walked the path of life and learned that wisdom and understanding become brighter as you walk further along the path. As young men, his sons are still walking at daybreak, when the light is just enough to illuminate the way ahead but not yet bright enough to show the whole journey. Solomon has been down the road and knows the light of "full day." Now he is symbolically coming back to encourage his sons to keep walking toward that light, because it will shine "brighter and brighter" for them as they keep walking in the way of wisdom until they reach the "full day" as he has.

Solomon clearly contrasts the choices he is presenting to his sons—they can walk on the "path of the righteous" (v. 18) or they can walk on the "way of the wicked" (v. 19). If they choose the latter, they will walk in darkness and won't even know what it is they are tripping over when they fall. If they walk in darkness, they will leave behind the guard that wisdom provides to keep them safe. This is the choice all believing parents know they are offering their children through their "discipline and instruction of the Lord" (Ephesians 6:4)—we want them to hold on to our teaching, to guard God's wisdom, and to choose to walk in the light of the path of righteousness.

We moved to rural central Texas when our children were young.

Our family property was two miles from the nearest town of 701 people and ten miles from the next closest town of 2,000. When we first started talking with our children about the path of life, we would occasionally take them out for a morning walk along our country road in the predawn quiet, stepping carefully to avoid rocks and cracks in the road we might stumble on in the dark. As the sun's light began to glow just below the horizon, our children could envision Solomon's imagery from Proverbs as the sky grew brighter and the road ahead became steadily more visible. They could understand, even at a young age, an otherwise abstract truth—that wisdom is like light in the darkness while walking on a long road, and the longer you walk, the brighter it becomes. This truth about wisdom and the contrast between light and dark provide a backdrop for what Solomon has to say in coming verses about guarding the heart for the journey.

⁓ ⁓

Solomon is about to pivot back to an admonition that will define this heartbeat of lifegiving parenting for guarding your child's heart. In verse 6 of chapter 4, he talked about how wisdom guards our lives; in verse 13, he talked about how we must guard wisdom because it is our life; and in verse 23, he'll talk about how we need to use wisdom to guard our hearts because it defines our lives.

Solomon prefaces what he is about to say with a personal directive enjoining his sons: "Keep [my words] in the midst of your heart. For they are life to those who find them" (vv. 21-22). Once again he uses a Hebrew word, translated here as "keep," that can also mean to guard or protect. And again this guarding of the heart is connected with life—not just physical life but also spiritual life. He's not telling his sons to wear breastplates on their chests to protect their physical hearts but rather to internalize his instruction to protect their spiritual hearts—to put a guard over their inner person—the combination of their minds, emotions, and wills that defines them.

What Solomon says next stands out as a pivotal truth at the heart of his advice to his sons: "Guard your heart above all else, for it determines the course of your life" (v. 23, NLT). What he instructs them to do for themselves as young men is what we also must do for our young children in order to guard *their* hearts. Here's an amplified paraphrase to make his words about that admonition clearer: "Guard and watch over your heart—the inner person that is the real you—like a guard who stands diligently on a wall." Some might wonder if Solomon is referring to what comes out of the heart or what comes into it. His word choice suggests the latter; after all, guards are placed on walls to keep threats out. But then he explains why that is important—because what comes into the heart will determine a person's "course of . . . life." He uses a Hebrew term (here translated "course") that suggests the farthest border of a piece of land or, in this context, the boundaries or limits of a person's life. Whatever comes into your children's hearts is what will define them and determine the course their lives take.

If wisdom and understanding go into your heart, then you will be on God's path—His wisdom will guard you (v. 6), you will guard it (v. 13), and by it you will guard the inner person of your heart (v. 23). You can anchor that principle in your mind with a more modern proverb: What goes into a heart comes out in a life. This is a critical principle when your children are young and still in their formative years, before their internal filters are fully "trained to discern good and evil" (Hebrews 5:14). Let good things in, and good things will come out; let bad things in, and bad things can come out. Jesus affirmed the same truth: "A good person produces good things from the treasury of a good heart, and an evil person produces evil things from the treasury of an evil heart. What you say flows from what is in your heart" (Luke 6:45, NLT). When you guard your children's hearts so they let wisdom and goodness in and keep folly and evil out, you not only direct them into God's life but also set their courses on paths of righteousness. It's all about helping them find and follow the life of God. That is lifegiving parenting, and there may be nothing more important for you as a lifegiving parent than guarding your children's hearts.

⤙ ⤚

So what does it look like to guard your children's hearts? What has changed in three thousand years since Solomon's words? I would have to agree with him that "there is nothing new under the sun" (Ecclesiastes 1:9). The reasons a guard is needed on the wall of your children's hearts are roughly the same now as when Solomon expressed the concept to his sons. Your children need your protection in three major areas: relationships, appetites, and influences. In the chapters that follow, we'll explore at length letting positives into the heart, but for now I want to talk briefly about being a lifegiving guard who protects your young children's vulnerable hearts from negatives before they reach young adulthood.

Relationships

Granted, the negative relationships Solomon warned against for young men—spending time with sinners, fools, and those who are violent, immoral, or wicked—are not what you worry about for your younger children. However, the way you guard your children's relationships in the early years can influence whether or not those darker issues end up on the relational radar when they are older. Remember, what goes into a heart comes out in a life, and that goes for relational experiences as well as wisdom.

One of Solomon's pithier proverbs about relationships should be a governing principle even in childhood: "He who walks with wise men will be wise, but the companion of fools will suffer harm"

(Proverbs 13:20). It's a straightforward affirmation of the importance of guarding relationships—one Sally and I committed to memory when our kids were young and quoted regularly to ourselves and especially to them. It wasn't just about us being protective parents but was also about them learning early the importance of choosing good, godly friends and avoiding those who were foolish and unwise.

However, our starting point for guarding our children's hearts was not about their relationships with others but about our relationships with them. We wanted to be the primary relational influence in their lives. We worked hard at relationship—not only as their parents who loved them, but also as their mentors and friends. By God's design, we already shared a parent-child relationship, but that was only a starting point for a lifelong bond as believers as well. Our goal was to be loving and grace-driven parents who would open and win our children's hearts. We would be the wisest and best companions in their lives.

When kids today have so many relationships—through the neighborhood, church, school, sports, activities, and even online—the responsibility to guard your children's relationships, and to build yours with them, can seem overwhelming. But both must be done, even if hard decisions and sacrifices are required, in order to protect them from foolish and unwise companions who could steer them away from you and God's path. Even a small deviation can become a large one as they get older.

Young children are not fools as described in Proverbs, but their adult parents and young-adult siblings certainly can be. The immature and untrained children of foolish parents can act foolishly and unwisely, reflecting their parents' misguided values and beliefs. Proverbs describes fools not only as naive, undisciplined, and ignorant but also as wicked, deceitful, and dangerous. There are simply too many ways that a foolish adult can harm your children—inappropriate exposure to sexuality, undesirable words and ideas, and even physical danger—for you not to vigorously exercise your role to protect their hearts from potential harm. That can happen through friends of your child who, by no fault of their own, are growing up without godly parents. In that case, always let your children know that your home is a safe place to bring any child, whatever their family situation may be. Don't discourage them from reaching out to other children who need a godly influence, yet at the same time guard their hearts from emotional attachments that could become a source of negative influences.

Wisdom is the ultimate protection your children need from you, and one expression of that is preventing them from being harmed, directly or indirectly, by foolish adults—those who do not or will not believe in God, who are amoral or immoral, and who are deliberately or unknowingly false teachers. Many of these people might be friends, coworkers, and neighbors, and their children may be your children's playmates, schoolmates, and companions. You may rightly want to be a witness for Christ or a positive influence on them and on their children. However, those biblical motivations must not be allowed to supersede your primary biblical responsibility to guard and protect your children's hearts. Even one spiritual, physical, or psychological wound can create a pothole in your path of parenting or, worse, life-long scars on your children's hearts. Remember that you are the wise one with whom you want your children to walk, and they need you to be wise in how you help them navigate their relationships.

Appetites

When we hear the word *appetite*, we naturally think of a physical need for food or a personal desire for certain kinds of foods—meats, pies, veggies, cakes, cheeses, breads. It is such a defining part of human experience that we've created the maxim "You are what you eat" to suggest that the kinds of foods our appetites cause us to put into our mouths will in some way define who we are. Appetite is given by God and is not a bad thing, but the way we control our appetites can affect our lives for either good or bad.

In Scripture, physical appetites are analogous to spiritual appetites— the desires that control our spiritual longings and choices. Jesus said, "Blessed are those who hunger and thirst for righteousness, for they shall be satisfied" (Matthew 5:6). Paul suggested that positive spiritual appetites start in the mind: "Set your mind on the things above, not on the things that are on earth" (Colossians 3:2). The apostle John warned about negative spiritual desires: "For all that is in the world, the lust of the flesh and the lust of the eyes and the boastful pride of life, is not from the Father, but is from the world" (1 John 2:16).

Children have appetites, just like adults, but with one big difference—they do not have the discipline and discernment at their young ages to control their appetites maturely. In the same way that parents naturally guard their children's physical appetites so their bodies will be healthy, we as believing parents must also guard our children's spiritual appetites so their hearts and spirits will be healthy. Solomon reminds us, "It is better to be content with what the eyes can see than for one's heart always to crave more" (Ecclesiastes 6:9, NET©), or, as the New International Version puts it, to have "the roving of the appetite." This is a good verse to remember as we attempt to train the appetites of our children, who are inundated with so many desirable choices that are always in front of them—media, movies, books, music, electronics, video games, amusements, activities, mobile apps, and experiences.

As parents, our best defense against appetites for things that will *not* feed our children the life of God is to train their appetites for the things that *will*. In Paul's words, "Whatever is true, whatever is honorable, whatever is right, whatever is pure, whatever is lovely, whatever is of good repute, if there is any excellence and if anything worthy of praise, dwell on these things" (Philippians 4:8). We'll talk more about this in chapter 5. But for now, we're considering the responsibility to guard our children's hearts against appetites that can lead them into things that are empty and lifeless or, much worse, into things that could subtly turn them from God. Training our children's appetites for the things that bring them into the life of God is a proactive process; training their appetites away from things that don't is reactive. In other words, when we see the danger, we must step in to guard and protect them.

Not all childhood appetites are neutral or innocent. Early appetites for "worldly things" might not lead into sin, but routinely indulging, ignoring, or excusing unhealthy childhood appetites can create a pattern that becomes a problem as our children get older. By being heart-guards who keep those appetites at bay when children are young and trainable, we can exercise for our children the mature discernment and self-denial that they do not yet possess. By preventing the negative, mediocre, and empty things of the world from capturing their appetites, we can make room for the positive, excellent, and lifegiving things. Sadly, some parents are good at preventing the bad but then are unwilling to provide something better—that which is excellent, ennobling, godly. They satiate their children's appetites with innocent but childish things that feed their immaturity rather than their developing maturity. Yet one of the more rewarding aspects of parenting is giving our children what is best for them and seeing them fix their hearts on what is good and ennobling.

But you won't become an effective lifegiving parent who both guards and trains your children's appetites unless you remember one thing: Your children will acquire appetites for the lifegiving things of God primarily because of what *you* value, *not* because of what you *want them* to value. If you want them to desire things that lead them to the life of God, then you will have to show them what that means by your own appetite choices for lifegiving media, music, reading, and all the rest. They need to see you applying Paul's list of "whatever" values to your appetites, not just using it to control theirs. That kind of positive modeling may be the most effective way you can guard your children's hearts.

Influences

Nathan was our "different" child (he tells his story in the book *Different*, cowritten with Sally). His mental battles would not have a name—OCD and ADD—until he was in his teens, but even in his childhood we began to see hints of what would make him unique. We didn't understand what we were seeing, but it was clear to us that whatever it was could have a strong influence on his heart and mind. It would have been easy, and even seen as normal by many Christian parents, for us to discipline his odd behavior strictly and demand conformity to social norms he didn't always follow. When we tried that approach, we found it at odds with our spirits, believing God wanted us simply to love our different child and try to understand the forces that were influencing his spirit. In order to guard his heart as he grew, it sometimes felt like we exercised more grace and patience with him than with all our other children combined. We just wanted him to have the same lifegiving upbringing as his siblings.

Guarding your children's hearts is all about protecting them from the negative forces that can shape their lives and prevent them from experiencing God's life—interpersonal forces (relationships), personal forces (appetites), and extrapersonal forces (influences). Of the three, it is the most difficult to see, much less to name, influences on your children's hearts that can wield a strong formative force on who they will become. As a lifegiving parent, guarding and protecting your children's hearts from the negative effects of those sometimes-mysterious influences will require your full-on attention and engagement. You'll need to be part sentinel, part sleuth, part shepherd, and part spiritual samurai—watching over, figuring out, caring about, and battling with the challenges of heart-shaping influences.

Exploring the breadth and depth of the many influences on your children would require a full-length book. The best I can hope for in a few paragraphs is to encourage you to be alert to the impact of negative influences on your children's hearts that can affect their relationships with you and God. Let me name just a few of the sources of influence that can quietly shape your children's hearts, minds, or spirits: personality, popular culture, personal passions, education, physical appearance, mental issues, medical issues, fears and insecurities, birth order, disabilities, skills and abilities, gender, and intellect. These kinds of influences are not by their natures bad; they are neutral on their own. However, any influence, or some aspect of it, can potentially develop into a source of negative thoughts and attitudes, and it is from those that you need to protect your children's hearts.

The reason you should be aware of what is influencing your children's hearts is simply because children are very influenceable. They do not have the maturity or discernment to understand or deal with every influence that comes into their lives. But you do. By the Holy Spirit within you, you can help your children make sense of what they are feeling or thinking and put it in the context of biblical truth. You can help them trust God, or you can trust God for them. You can also discern an influence that is creating unhealthy attitudes or beliefs and provide instruction to counter them. It is simply another way to guard your children's hearts—keep out the bad and let in the good.

One last thing. Influences can sometimes be big and scary challenges for any parent. If they have a negative impact on your children's hearts, the effects can be subtle, difficult to understand, and hidden from view, and they can even seem out of your control. Before your children are able to make sense of them, they will be more likely to listen to your parental love, patience, and counsel. But sometimes, especially in preteen and early teen years when hormonal changes can distort perceptions and feelings, the influences will generate frustrating episodes of immaturity, anger, and irrationality that will seem impervious to your mature insight and parental wisdom. A proverb I found useful for applying to all of my children's influences was "Trust in the LORD with all your heart and do not lean on your own understanding. In all your ways acknowledge Him, and He will make your paths straight" (Proverbs 3:5-6). God is trustworthy and is committed to helping you guard your children's hearts to give them His life.

⋩ ⋫

As a lifegiving parent, you are the guardian and protector of your children's hearts, directing them away from "the way of the wicked" (Proverbs 4:19) and onto "the ancient paths, where the good way is" (Jeremiah 6:16). Your job as a heart guard is not complicated—it is to keep your children on God's "good way" and path of life so they will know and experience the very life of God in your home and family. That path is as old as the Bible's story and as new as the latest relationships, appetites, or influences looking for a place in your children's hearts. You are the gate that either opens to let them in or closes to keep them out, depending on which path brings them to your children.

Throughout Scripture, the people of God have been continually confronted with binary choices between God and the world, good and evil, life and death. Moses said, "I have set before you life and death, the blessing and the curse. So choose life in order that you may live" (Deuteronomy 30:19). Solomon contrasted the "path of the righteous" and the "way of the wicked" (Proverbs 4:18-19). Psalmists and prophets declared the choice. Jesus said, "No one can serve two masters. . . . You cannot serve God and wealth" (Matthew 6:24). Paul, John, and Peter laid out the choices between darkness and light, law and grace, right and wrong, bondage and freedom, flesh and Spirit, works and faith, old self and new self, the world and the Word, and many others. We all have to choose a way.

But as citizens of a new Kingdom and followers of "the Way" (Acts 9:2), our choice is no longer only about a path but is also about a person. Jesus declared Himself to be the embodiment of that ancient but always present choice when He said, "I am the way, and the truth, and the life; no one comes to the Father but through Me" (John 14:6). Or even more emphatically, "I am the way, even the truth and the life" (NET©; see translators' note). He called Himself the path of life to God when He declared to crowds of Jews at the feast in Jerusalem, "I am the Light of the world; he who follows Me will not walk in the darkness, but will have the Light of life" (John 8:12).

Why is this important? Because you're guarding your children's hearts so they will find not just a better way of life, but the true Way who is the life. You're guarding their hearts not just so some of your Jesus-light will shine on them, but so they will walk with Jesus, who is the Light. You're guarding their hearts not just so they can live better, but so they will come to know and experience the life of God that is found only in Jesus, the Light of the world, who said, "I came that they may have life, and have it abundantly" (John 10:10). He is the true "life" that you are giving to them.

When you step onto your path of parenting, as *Just David*'s father did, you are beginning a journey to lead your children into the best life you can give them—life with God, who has come to walk with us as Jesus through His Spirit. As you guard your children's hearts on that journey with them, you will as a follower of Christ open their eyes to life that will never end. That's the ultimate joy of lifegiving parenting.

Sally's Lifegiving Memoirs

When our boys, Joel and Nathan, were around seven and nine, I was very aware of trying to cultivate good spiritual appetites in them. It was a time in boyhood when they could have easily been pulled into many competing appetites for worldly things—or just empty things. One decision we made to protect their developing appetites was not to let them watch Saturday morning cartoons.

One Friday I had been showing them some beautiful English artwork, and we had looked at one painting of two boys behind a barracks, playing cards while soldiers trained. We talked about what story the painting was trying to tell, what the boys might have been like, and what it means to be a soldier during wartime.

The next day, Saturday, I had let them spend some time with friends in a nearby town. As we were driving home, Joel asked me, "Mommy, why aren't we allowed to watch Saturday morning cartoons like our friends?" We talked about what cartoons they had watched at their friends' house and what they were like.

When we got home, I took out some paper and scribbled a simple stick-figure drawing of two boys. I asked, "What do you think of my drawing? Is it beautiful? Is it interesting? What kind of story is it telling?"

Joel said, "Mama, it isn't interesting at all and doesn't have a story. I could draw better than that."

I asked, "Well, why was the painting we talked about yesterday interesting to you?"

He responded, "Well, because it had real people, and color. I could imagine the two boys in it being Nathan and me. It told an interesting story."

I said, "That's exactly right. And do you know why you were able to appreciate those things? Because I've tried to feed your mind the very best mind foods I can. It's just like real food. I don't let you eat junk food and sugars because of what I know they will do to your body. In the same way, I don't let you watch the junk food and sugars of Saturday morning cartoons because of what I know they will do to your mind and spirit. I want to feed your mind with good things so you'll have a healthy mind and imagination to create things like the painting of the two boys."

It's one of the Clarkson stories that has come down through the years. It was an important lesson—not just for our children but also for their parents. God doesn't want us to let mediocrity crowd out excellence in our minds; He wants us to train our appetites to appreciate beauty and excellence.

Lifegiving ParenTips

Discerning lasting versus passing. Part of guarding your child's heart against negative input is knowing when to react and when to respond. The difference is whether the matter acting on your child's heart could be of lasting (permanent) or passing (temporary) impact. If it's something that you discern could leave a long-term negative imprint (violent movie scene, bad language, horror images) or possibly even a spiritual wound (sexual or pornographic content), then you need to react—step in quickly and forcefully to protect your child's heart. If it's something you perceive could make a short-term negative imprint (scary kids' movie, embarrassing situation, rough playmate), then you can respond—intervene if necessary, but don't overreact and make the matter worse than it is. You don't want to be a helicopter parent, always hovering fearfully over your child, but you do want to be the always-ready jet pilot, ready to dive in when the right stuff is needed.

Parenting proactively. The emphasis in this chapter is more on reactive and responsive parenting to guard your child's heart from the bad things that could get in. However, the best defense can be a good offense—making sure you're letting lots of the good stuff into your child's heart so it can squeeze out the bad stuff. That's proactive parenting—being a proactively positive protector of your child's heart. For relationships, that might mean finding good and godly friends for your child to play with; making your home an inviting, fun, and safe place where your child and others want to come; and even making more time as parents to be with your child. For appetites, that will mean providing a great library of good books; exposing your children to a variety of good music (not just childish music); carefully choosing a restricted diet of quality videos, apps, and screen-oriented amusements; and giving your children a wide exposure to new skills, hobbies, instruments, and more. For influences, it will mean creating a verbal home where anyone can talk about anything with you; expanding your children's life experiences with you; and exploring their personalities, skills, and passions.

Supernatural isn't always super. We live in a culture awash in science fiction, science fantasy, and spiritual fantasy, not to mention superheroes of every imaginable kind. There seems to be no age barrier for most of these kinds of movies anymore, so if all your children's friends are seeing the latest blockbuster, your children will want to see it too. Before giving up and giving in, though, consider your children's tolerance for what they'll be seeing and whether or not it's something that you feel is right for them at their ages. Stories about intelligent life from other planets, UFOs and aliens, or occult or supernatural elements can be confusing and disturbing to some children, while not really affecting others. You won't be a bad parent if you, discerning your children's spirits, simply delay viewing those films until they're older. In fact, you may be the best kind of parent, guarding their hearts.

Starting the Heartbeat of Parental Lifegiving

Guarding your child's heart starts with setting boundaries to protect and defend. When you guard your child's relationships, appetites, and influences, you will let wisdom and goodness in and keep evil and folly out to set your child's course in life.

CHAPTER 5

RENEWING YOUR CHILD'S MIND

*Do not be conformed to this world, but be transformed by the
renewing of your mind, so that you may prove what the will
of God is, that which is good and acceptable and perfect.*

ROMANS 12:2

IT'S SAFE TO SAY that most of us would agree with the popular aphorism "A mind is a terrible thing to waste." That unforgettable phrase
first entered the collective American mind in 1972 as the slogan
for UNCF ads, helping that worthy organization raise billions of
dollars in scholarships for African American college students. It has
since become part of the American vernacular, expressing a truth that
resonates for all thinking people: Every mind is valuable and worthy
of investment and development. It also suggests that the mind is a
renewable resource, or, as Leonardo da Vinci quipped (though not
in English), "Learning never exhausts the mind." In other words, the
more we invest in the mind, the more it will give back.

Those ideas shaped the mind-affirming atmosphere we deliberately set out to create in our home. In fact, I'm certain we intoned
the phrase "A mind is a terrible thing to waste" to our children more
than a few times over the years. When we did, it was not to inflict

guilt but to incite enthusiasm—to engage their nascent and developing curiosity and their drive to know more. We endeavored to create a positive learning attitude by presenting learning as something exciting and enjoyable, not just for them but for us as adults, too. We entered parenthood knowing that it would be our responsibility to set the pattern and pace for our children's mental development, and we kept that commitment to nurture their minds throughout our years of parenting.

To be clear, our mind-affirming efforts were not about schooling. Our deepest conviction was that the most important learning for our children would not be what happened in a classroom but what transpired in the informal settings of our home. We've taught families for thirty years that no matter where their children's formal education happens—public school, private school, home—the real development of their children's minds will happen in the home and family, which God has designed to be the primary location for children's mental growth. We homeschooled, and yet we knew that our children's formal learning was very different from the learning that God meant to happen naturally in the real-life settings with us in our home. That's where the lifegiving parenting of renewing our children's minds would happen.

In the spirit of Moses' mandate for Israel in the Shema that directed families to diligently teach their children (see chapter 1), we looked for opportunities to train our children's brains—while sitting at home or out walking, going to bed and getting up (see Deuteronomy 6:4-9). But there was one place while "sitting at home" that we especially saw as our mind-making time—the family table. In her book *The Lifegiving Table*, Sally explores how the table was in many ways the heart of our family life, the place where as followers of Christ we engaged in "the renewing of [the] mind" of our children. We resonate with Leonard Sweet in his book *From Tablet to Table*: "For Jesus the home is not what defines the table; the table is what defines the home."[1]

The table is a uniquely and, in ways explained in Sally's book, divinely ordered part of family life for the spiritual influence of children. Think about the family table for a moment. There is a physical unity when all sit at the table together, infused with the experiential unity of sharing a meal together. That dynamic fosters a naturally interactive setting—looking at each other, engaging in conversation, serving one another. Taken all together, the table creates an anchor, a way for family members to be together. We tried to take full advantage of those times at our table to challenge our children's thinking, encourage their expression of ideas and opinions, talk about current events of the day, explore theological views and Bible knowledge, talk about relationships, and so much more. Whenever there was food on the table, we also put food for the mind there.

And whenever we could, we ate at the table together. We simply refused to give in to the American norm that considers meals as little more than necessary fueling stops between other more important activities. According to some statistics, the average time spent at a dinner table has shrunk from ninety minutes in the middle of the last century to less than twelve minutes today—enough time to eat and run, but certainly not to discuss and engage. The popular television police procedural *Blue Bloods* provides a picture of commitment to the family table that is noteworthy because it is such an uncommon experience for most families.

That fictional picture of the Reagan family dynamic is very familiar to the Clarkson family. When we were at the table, we were talking. When our children were younger, we would read the Bible and talk about the characters and the meaning of the passages. We would talk about God, Jesus, the Christian life, faith, love, and whatever topics our children would find interesting. As they got older, we would talk about theological issues, books we'd read, stories in the news, biblical standards for relationships, ministry ideas—ad infinitum. There was also an abundance of lighthearted banter, debates about the best musical artists and songs, analyses of movies, sharing interesting or funny YouTube videos and blog posts, and so much more. With so much talking going on between the eating, our meals sometimes actually approached that ninety-minute experience from last century.

We always worked to take seriously the apostle Paul's convictions about the mind. Yet while I feel confident that Paul would have resonated with the saying "A mind is a terrible thing to waste," I'm also fairly certain he would have felt it was an incomplete statement. Paul was not so concerned with the mind as an organ of human thinking and making the brain better so we don't waste our mental capabilities. Paul was concerned with our spiritual mind, the quality of our inner person that enables us to believe in Jesus, love and obey God, love others, understand biblical truth, assess error, resist sin and choose righteousness, and do God's will. He was concerned that we understand, strengthen, and renew "the mind of Christ" (1 Corinthians 2:16) that we have as believers. Why? Because that is where the life of Christ is found—the life within us.

And that's why renewing your children's minds is a heartbeat of lifegiving parenting—it's about bringing them into contact with the life of Christ through the mind. Depending on your children's ages, you may be providing that through a kind of surrogate experience—letting them see and experience through you the mind renewal Paul describes. The older they are, the more you'll be providing a modeling experience—helping them understand what it means to renew the mind as a believer and how to keep it renewed. In order to understand how this works, we'll need to spend some time in Romans 12:1-2. What we'll find there is a critical two-verse description of what it means to renew the mind as a disciple of Christ.

❧ ❦

Paul's letter to the church in Rome is his magnum opus of the new covenant, explaining what God has done in Christ to redeem a people for Himself. In chapters 1–11, Paul narrates the transcendent truths about fallen humanity, the saving work of Christ, and the sovereignty of God working through Israel. In chapters 12–16, he explores our service as Christians to the church and the world. Between those two sections is the hinge of Romans 12:1-2. In those two powerful verses, Paul addresses our *response* to God (offering our lives to Him) and our *responsibility* to God (living our lives for Him). If we or our kids miss this critical hinge passage, we can miss the point of the whole story Paul is telling in Romans. Here's the text:

> Therefore I urge you, brethren, by the mercies of God, to present your bodies a living and holy sacrifice, acceptable to God, which is your spiritual service of worship. And do not be conformed to this world, but be transformed by the renewing of your mind, so that you may prove what the will of God is, that which is good and acceptable and perfect.

First, in verse 1, Paul thinks back on everything God has done for us (chapters 1–11) and concludes that the reasonable response to His many mercies is to offer our lives—literally, our bodies—to Him in worship. In contrast to the dead sacrifices offered by Jewish priests in the Temple, which are intended to purify the one making the offering, Paul says we are already "living and holy" sacrifices in Christ. Not only will we be "acceptable" to God (see Romans 14:16-18), we're able to present ourselves to God—to lay ourselves down on His altar. It's the same offering Paul refers to earlier in his letter when he enjoins believers to "present yourselves to God as those alive from the dead" (6:13). This is where lifegiving parenting begins—with your "spiritual service of worship" offered to God. And this is where the renewing of your mind and your children's minds begins—at the cross of Christ.

Then, in verse 2, Paul looks ahead to what we must do for God (chapters 12–16). He makes it very clear that there is nothing passive about our life with Him. It's not enough to simply say, "Here I am, Lord" and then wait for God to do something. Once we offer ourselves to God, we must then say, "Here I go, Lord" and move forward by faith. So Paul gives two commands to show how that is going to happen: We must stop being conformed, and we must start being transformed. We stop letting the world tell us how to think, and we start renewing our minds to think like Christ. This is how we will show that we are doing the will of God. If we want the life of God in our homes for our children—if we're serious about being lifegiving parents—then following both of these commands is nonnegotiable.

The first command to "not be conformed to this world" is negative, telling us what not to do. Paul is essentially shouting, "Stop letting the times in which you live shape how you think!" A bit more literally, Paul is telling us to stop allowing the culture to etch (*syschēmatizō*) its beliefs into our brains like an unseen draftsman drawing a schematic, or pattern, of the culture's beliefs onto our neural pathways. The word for "world" is *aiōn*, which does not mean the world system but the period of time in which we live. The Roman believers lived in a different time than we do, but the command applies to us equally. Paul is saying that we must make a conscious choice to stop being influenced by the "isms" that define our particular time—in our case, relativism, materialism, postmodernism, spiritualism, hedonism, atheism, whateverism. Redeeming our minds as parents, and our children's minds, starts with some serious stopping.

The second command is positive and goes right to the heart of this lifegiving parent heartbeat: "Be transformed by the renewing of your mind." Instead of being passively conformed to the world, Paul commands us to actively let God transform our minds. The Greek word he uses, *metamorphoō*, should sound familiar to you and your kids if you've ever used morphing software to combine two faces (or, even better, a human face and an animal one). It's the same metamorphosis Paul describes in 2 Corinthians 3:18, of Christians "being *transformed* into [Christ's] image with ever-increasing glory" (NIV, emphasis added). How does this transformation occur? It happens when we choose to renew our minds—to make our conformed thinking "new again" with God's truth. Paul doesn't directly mention Scripture as the source of that renewal, but it's clear from his reference to "the will of God" that this is what he has in mind. "To renew" means exactly what you think it should—to make new by the Spirit.

Since renewing the mind is the spiritual juice that makes transformation happen, we also need to get a better mental handle on what Paul means by "the mind." He uses the term *nous*, which, along with its derivatives, primarily "focuses on ability to grasp and understand the revealed will of God."[2] Paul admonishes believers elsewhere to no longer walk "in the futility of their mind" as nonbelievers do but rather to "be renewed in the spirit of your mind" (Ephesians 4:17, 23) and to "set your mind on the things above, not on the things that are on earth" (Colossians 3:2). The mind that Paul is talking about is "the mind of Christ" that we all have as believers.

Finally, Paul wraps up verse 2 by declaring the purpose of being "transformed by the renewing of your mind." It isn't just to be spiritual or to please God, although it is certainly both; it is also to prove that His will is genuine and good, the real thing in a corrupt world. The NIV gets closer to this idea: "Then you will be able to *test and approve* what God's will is—his good, pleasing and perfect will" (emphasis added). And "perfect" (*teleios*) might be better translated as "complete" or "whole." God's will is everything it is meant to be and to accomplish.

That was a close look, but it was necessary to help us understand what renewing our children's minds is all about. The underlying reality of Romans 12:1-2 is that there is no life in Christ without a transformed and renewed mind. In the New Testament, the renewed and Spirit-infused mind is the only mind that counts—it's the only mind that has the life of God. And as a lifegiving parent, you cannot bring the life of God into your home without a renewed mind. Whatever stages of maturity your children may be at right now, it's your mind and your spouse's mind that will be able to "prove" for them that God's will is "good and acceptable and perfect."

As we step back from that close look, let's refocus on ways to make this passage come alive in your home.

❧ ❧

If you haven't already figured this out, Romans 12:1-2 is a favorite Bible passage of mine. The more I studied it, the more I discovered in its fifty Greek words, and the more I uncovered in its threaded connections to numerous biblical truths about the Christian life. It packs a lot into a few words. Through the years, one of the ways I've taught these two verses is as "The Signs of a Disciple." I identified four signs of being a disciple of Christ that can correlate with the universal experience of driving a car. I hope the four signs will capture the content of the passage in a way that will be memorable, meaningful, and useful for you and your children. The signs are YIELD to God, STOP the World, GO to the Word, and SHOW the Way. Let's take a drive with this passage.

YIELD to God

Renewing your child's mind at home starts with the idea of yielding, or presenting, your life to God. The etymological picture behind the word translated "present" (yield) is to "stand with"—we physically, with our bodies, "stand with" Jesus. It's a concrete image of the abstract idea that we owe our allegiance to Christ. True faith in Christ is not just mental assent or belief; it is also physical allegiance. That kind of "stand with" Jesus faith is demonstrated best by parents who don't just talk about spiritual things but also live out their relationships with the Lord.

Paul calls the idea of yielding to God our "spiritual service of worship." In other words, if we are truly presenting (yielding) our lives to Christ, then it is reasonable for us to respond with service and worship (see James 1:22-24). So one thing we can do at home, as a starting place for our children, is to express our worship of God together as a family. Worship at home is probably not something that happens naturally for most families; it can certainly be for some an awkward and stressful experience. Realistically, if it's not part of the family culture throughout the year, the words "we're going to do family worship now" probably will not induce smiles. But you can work up to that without scaring the kids.

We found holidays were the easiest way to introduce worship into our family culture. For example, the Advent season (the four weekends leading up to Christmas Eve) and Christmas were full of opportunities. At the small-worship end of the spectrum, we would have a weekly Advent wreath candle-lighting time together around the table. Our ceremony would include Advent Scripture readings and discussions, perhaps a story, singing a couple of seasonal songs, and of course hot chocolate and a treat. Our shepherds' meal on Christmas Eve—a simple family dinner of thick potato soup, rustic bread, cheese, fruits, and nuts—was also a time for reading Scripture and responding to God. At the bigger-worship end of the spectrum, we had an annual festive event the week before Christmas for our family and friends. It would conclude with readings of Scripture, singing Christmas hymns and carols, and perhaps even a candlelit rendition of "Silent Night." We involved all of our children in planning, hosting, and participating.

We did similar events for other holidays, which made the non-holiday times of family worship seem like a natural part of our home's rhythms and culture. Worshiping together at church provided a similar kind of experience. Were they all times of "renewing the mind"? Not so much in the sense of learning, thinking, and talking about

God's Word but definitely in the sense that they provided practice for learning to yield to God and to "stand with" Jesus in worship. Only when we turn our children's hearts in the right direction will their minds be ready to be renewed.

STOP the World

When our children were young, the idea of conforming to the world for them was mostly about childish materialism, Disney-fied escapism, and "me first" kid hedonism. However, occasionally even our young children would have doubts and ideas that seemed to reflect the world's thinking. As they got older and began to be exposed to other worldviews and philosophies, we often needed to talk through the various "isms" that challenged their Christian beliefs. It was a strong reminder to us that Paul's admonition to stop being conformed to the time in which we live is primarily directed to us as parents, not to our children. If Sally and I were conformed to any of the world's isms, how could we ever be a godly influence and protect our children from them?

When the kids were young, we were diligent to protect their innocence from the crudity, violence, and sexuality of secular culture, and yet we came to realize that unless we hermetically sealed our home, we could not prevent worldly isms from getting into our children's minds. It was like *The Truman Show*, a Jim Carrey movie we all enjoyed. Truman, a young man in his twenties, is born and raised in a bubble-encased "world" that is actually a giant television set for a 24/7/365 show where, unknown to him, his family, friends, and community are all actors. The movie tells the story of how Truman figures out that his world is not real and then escapes, even as the evil producer of the show controls obstacles in an attempt to prevent him. At its heart, it is the story of the human spirit that will seek truth even when it is concealed and controlled. Sally and I did not want to create that kind of controlled home from which our children would one day want to escape. We wanted a home where we, as lifegiving parents, could engage ideas with them and prepare them to become nonconforming Christians in the world, with minds renewed by the Spirit of Christ.

If we were to keep the life of Christ alive in our home for our children, it meant we had to be both reactive and proactive. First, we had to be reactive if we recognized any ways that we, and especially our teen children, were being subtly influenced by the world's isms, allowing our thinking patterns to follow a way of thinking that did not reflect God's truth. For instance, relativism, the idea that truth is not absolute, might have crept into someone's thinking about an ethical issue not addressed directly by Scripture. Or postmodernism, with its skepticism and distrust of metanarratives like those that define much of Christian belief, and its drive to deconstruct traditional ways of thinking, might have shown up in our kids' words as we discussed church or family structures and experience.

Though we would react when our biblical beliefs were challenged, we were not reactionary. We would first engage our children's ideas and discuss them, and then we would confront and correct error with the teachings of Scripture. We were not alarmed by the ideas our children would hear but were confident and direct in correcting them with God's truth. We followed Paul's strategy with the Corinthian church, which was also awash in isms and unbiblical beliefs: "We demolish arguments and every pretension that sets itself up against the knowledge of God, and *we take captive every thought to make it obedient to Christ*" (2 Corinthians 10:5, NIV; emphasis added). We would not allow unbiblical ideas to go unchallenged but would confidently "take captive" every such thought and bring it into submission under a Christ-centered view of life and reality.

It was rare that we needed to be reactive, but that may be because we also put concerted effort into being proactive—thoughtfully deflecting future issues about isms by helping our children understand

Christianity as an intellectually and philosophically defensible view of the world. We never shied away from those kinds of discussions when our kids brought them up, but more importantly, we regularly initiated them. If there was a controversial issue in a popular book, movie, or song, we would have our children, even before their teens, look up different views about the issue, and then we would have a family discussion. Or more commonly, if there was a significant current event in the news—conflicts, politics, social issues, media, technology, science—we would all read about it and then discuss how we should think about the issue from a biblical perspective. Being deliberate about countering the influences of the time in which we live will help us renew our minds, and our children's.

GO to the Word

This is the most comfortable of the four signs, yet not always the easiest to follow. Paul commands us as believers to "be transformed by the renewing of your mind," and that renewal comes from God's Word. However, keep in mind two caveats about his command. First, "be transformed" is about a process, not an event. It's not a one-and-done task that never needs to be completed again. It's gradual and ongoing, not instantaneous. Second, "renewing of your mind" is about a living organism, not a programmable computer. That's where the "living and active" (Hebrews 4:12) Word of God comes in.

Part of going to the Word of God to renew your children's minds is beginning with a reality check of what the Bible is and is not and what it does and does not do. The Bible is not a magical book that will change your children if you only apply a few choice verses or read the story of a relevant Bible character. Nor is it a textbook for Christian living to be learned only for Sword Drills, Bible club, and Sunday school quizzes. It is especially not a source of God-words for you to use to inject guilt, shame, or fear into your children's minds. It helps to remember how the Bible refers to itself:

The word of God is living and active and sharper than any
two-edged sword, and piercing as far as the division of soul
and spirit, of both joints and marrow, and able to judge the
thoughts and intentions of the heart.

HEBREWS 4:12

Every scripture is inspired by God and useful for teaching,
for reproof, for correction, and for training in righteousness,
that the person dedicated to God may be capable and
equipped for every good work.

2 TIMOTHY 3:16-17, NET©

The Bible is God's revelation to us, revealing His heart and mind
so we can know Him, and His ways and will so we can please Him.
His inspired (God-breathed) Word changes us through His Holy
Spirit, allowing us to be useful in His service. His "living and active"
Word convicts us and guides us because the Spirit of God works
through the words of God. For all these reasons, the Bible is what can
renew our minds—make us new—and transform us into the likeness
of Jesus. It is not just what we will use as parents but also what God
will use through us to renew our children's minds.

God's Word permeated our home. We had numerous Bibles in
easy reach, Scripture calligraphy on the walls, Bible stories on the
bookshelves, Scripture-based devotions on coffee tables, Bible studies
and tools in the library. So when a question about a belief, worldview,
or philosophical idea came up and we wanted to know what the Bible
had to say, it did not require a major shift in focus to open a Bible
or Scripture resource and dive in. But from a proactive perspective,
going directly to Scripture when we had a question also trained our
children to know how to open the Bible, use a concordance, find a
commentary or topical study, or read a word study on their own.
In the days before ubiquitous Bible-study websites, we had some

Bible-study software, but our children's ability to use printed tools has been a life-shaping skill. Knowing God's Word and knowing how to learn from it can keep our children's minds renewed so they keep following Him.

SHOW the Way

The final sign is like the big green directional signs on the highway that help lead you to your destination. They show the way ahead. If you have yielded your life to God to serve and worship Him, stopped letting the world tell you how and what to think, and started going to the Word of God to renew your mind with truth, then your life should consequently become living proof that you're headed in the right direction—that the will of God is "good and acceptable and perfect." That's the endgame in the whole process of renewing your mind as a parent and renewing your child's mind—to show that God's way is the real way. But let's be clear on what Paul is saying. The proof of God's will is not in the yielding, stopping, and starting; those are the preliminaries. The proof that His will is good and perfect is when, *after* you yield, stop, and start, you then live in a way that shows the goodness of God's will.

This sign is where the proverbial rubber of the Word meets the road of life. But here again, to extend the driving metaphor, you as a parent are still in the driver's seat. Either your children are watching how you drive or you're teaching them how to drive. In other words, this particular sign is about your showing your children what the way and will of God look like. Paul even adds a personal pronoun for emphasis: "so that *you* may prove what the will of God is." The term for "prove" (*dokimazō*) means to test something in order to show that it is genuine. In this case, you are to test the will of God to show that it's the real thing, that it's where real life is found. And by your model as a lifegiving parent, you'll also be renewing your children's minds. How? By showing them—proving—that the Word of God is more than just words *about* God. It's the "living and active" Word of God that brings His life to you and to your home so you can follow His way and will. It's the real thing, bringing new life to your children.

Our children would see and participate in this proving process when Sally and I were faced with a difficult challenge, choice, or change that would require our faith and trust in God—such as a move to a new city, a lack of funds, a ministry opportunity, or a difficult relationship. Whenever possible, we engaged our children as we reviewed Scriptures for wisdom, considered what God would have us choose to do, and prayed about it. We were using our transformed spirits and renewed minds in order to "prove what the will of God" would be for us and to see it as "good and acceptable and perfect." And that pattern would then be repeated for matters of faith and trust that our children faced—friends, fears, desires, or decisions. Our model of showing the way by using our renewed minds provided a pattern they could follow to practice what a mature renewed mind would do. And through it all, we were asking the living God to be with us.

⊰ ⊱

Of all the heartbeats of lifegiving parenting, this one—renewing your children's minds—arguably requires the most from you as the parent. Your children, whether they are young and immature or beginning to mature as young teens, will be looking to you not just to understand what it means to have a redeemed mind but also to see what it means to live out of a redeemed mind. You are living out the spirit of Paul's admonition for them: "Follow my example, as I follow the example of Christ" (1 Corinthians 11:1, NIV). In many ways, your mature example of having a redeemed mind will serve as their first opportunity to practice what it means to be a disciple of Christ—to follow the way of God and do His will. If they don't see the life of God being lived out in you and are not encouraged to follow that example, their minds will likely be filled with other isms and appetites that will shape their own lives but not steer them to life in God.

Remember the aphorism that started this chapter? "A mind is a terrible thing to waste." Paul might have restated it more like this: "A Christian mind is a terrible thing not to renew." That version will make sense to you only when you have a clear understanding of what Paul says to all believers in Romans 12:1-2. If you understand the importance of each of the four "signs of a disciple" from that passage, and that they all stand together or fall apart, then you'll have a better picture for how to bring the life of God into your home for your children. Few of us as parents will do it as consistently and effectively as we'd like, but the important thing is your children will see God's life in you as lifegiving parents. In the process of yielding to God, stopping the world, going to the Word, and showing the way, you'll be renewing their minds. And then you'll never have to worry about wasted minds in your home.

Sally's Lifegiving Momoirs

Sometimes "out of the mouths of babes" has been the unexpected reality in our home. It was a Sunday evening during the first year in our new home in Monument, Colorado. I was doing the dishes after dinner and heard the familiar sounds of a heated discussion coming from the dining room. At first, I heard the three older children's voices engaged in a vigorous debate about a popular children's film they had watched together at their friend's house. As I came in and joined the good-natured fray, it soon became a girls-versus-boys debate, with me joining Team Sarah, and Clay joining the boys. Four-year-old Joy was quietly taking it all in.

Fourteen-year-old Sarah felt there were philosophical issues in the movie that could influence children with misleading and unbiblical ideas; the boys felt it was just a fun movie and the issues were not a big deal. We all talked with our usual fervor about the merits of the film, movie messages, and the potential influence of films on children. Seeing no quick resolution, I said I needed to put Joy in bed and they could figure it all out themselves. But as I headed down the stairs to Joy's room, so did everyone else, continuing the debate all the way into her bedroom. As the whole family was either standing around or sitting on her bed, and I was trying vainly to get her under the covers, Joy finally had enough. She stood up on her bed with feet spread apart, put both arms up in the air, closed her eyes, and said with great conviction, "Everybody stop! Take a deep breath, and think about Jesus!"

That did it. The words out of our babe's mouth put an end to the debate, bringing a surprised pause followed by tension-relieving laughter. But she was exactly right about the need of that moment. Joy was feisty and fierce even as a young child, with her own opinions about faith and serious insights about life. Even though she was not always able to enter into her siblings' discussions, she was always taking it all in, and her mind was being renewed just by being in the very verbal environment of our home. Every day, of course, she engaged in devotions and discussions of Scripture, and she heard many books read aloud and discussed, but she was also hearing the thoughtful opinions, passionate convictions, and logical arguments of the "big kids," which were feeding and forming her young mind. It's no big surprise that she ended up competing in speech and debate.

Lifegiving ParenTips

Read mind-renewing stories. Renewing your child's mind doesn't just involve reading and talking about the Bible. The Word of

God is crucial, but other "renewables" can work synergistically with the Word to renew the mind. Read stories of great men and women of faith from history and of God's work in and through His church around the world over the past two thousand years. Read the inspiring testimonies of ministers and missionaries, the history of the Bible and its worldwide impact on countless cultures of all nations and languages. Read the writings of church fathers and godly men and women, their devotionals and inspirational messages. Read the sermons of great preachers. All these and more are examples of learning from and being encouraged in faith by the great "cloud of witnesses surrounding us" (Hebrews 12:1)—all those who have gone before us. They bring the mind-renewing life of God to us in a timeless fellowship of faith.

Plan your table talk. When families meet over a delicious meal at the table, it is natural for children to resist any efforts by parents to formalize that special time. There is an organic, spontaneous, and natural quality to the interaction around the family table that can be lost, or at least greatly hindered, by parental efforts to control family discussion or turn the table into a classroom. And yet if there is no plan for how to make that time meaningful, the danger is that it can quickly degenerate into a random discussion of disconnected subjects. Your challenge as a lifegiving parent is twofold: (1) to plan some topics or questions that will help you direct the table conversation, and (2) to know how to guide conversation in a natural, informal way. For instance, if you want to talk about faith, don't announce it. Instead, ask a creative, thought-stimulating question that will segue into the real topic (e.g., "What do you believe *could* be true about Narnia?"). Also, learn how to ask for opinions rather than always giving your own. You don't need to correct most misguided ideas; instead, affirm your children for being insightful and thoughtful. Humor and interesting stories will always keep the conversation going.

Don't hide your example. Your parental example and model for your children will be the most effective way to renew their minds; they will learn by watching, learning from, and following your example. However, much of the Christian life, especially for introverts, tends to be private and unseen—personal Bible reading, devotional or quiet times, personal prayer, fellowship with a friend, listening to sermons or podcasts, reading inspiring books and blog posts, meditating, and more. The result is that much of your good example of how you renew your mind can be inadvertently hidden from your children. To overcome that detriment, develop the habit of sharing with your children the mind-renewing things you do that they don't see. Share with them what you learned from Scripture in your quiet time, what and who you prayed for, an inspiring story you found online or a book you're reading, or something the Lord is convicting your spirit about. It's a lifegiving parent habit.

Starting the Heartbeat of Parental Lifegiving

Renewing your child's mind starts with thoughtfully considering the mind of Christ. Keeping your child's mind renewed and growing for God means following the biblical traffic signs to stop the world's influence and go to the Word to find renewing truth.

CHAPTER 6

STRENGTHENING YOUR CHILD'S FAITH

Jesus said, "Let the children alone, and do not hinder them
from coming to Me; for the kingdom of heaven belongs to such as these."
MATTHEW 19:14

IT WAS A BEAUTIFUL DAY on the north shore of the Sea of Galilee. As the afternoon sun descended toward the Mediterranean, the shadows of the low limestone homes in the small town of Capernaum began to lengthen. Jesus sat on a smooth rock outcropping overlooking the inland lake crowded with fishing boats. The children from town were playing near the water, knowing the day would soon be gone. Jesus loved their childish laughter and frivolity, and he smiled at them, teased them, and laughed with them as they ran by. Their free-spirited innocence stirred longings in His own spirit for the Kingdom of Heaven He had first preached along that shore after returning from forty days in the wilderness. He closed His eyes, listened to the children, and imagined the Kingdom had come in all its fullness.

Above the happy childish din, he heard other older voices behind Him growing louder. Jesus reluctantly opened His eyes and looked back over His shoulder. He smiled upon seeing the fishing village

He now called home sitting peacefully in the rolling hills. He could see the synagogue where He first taught the town's people and they responded with amazement and faith. In Nazareth, His child-hood home, they had rejected His prophetic messages, and their lack of belief prevented Him from doing miracles there. But here in Capernaum, He had found a generous and welcoming faith, and He had healed and delivered many people. He had called His first disciples here—Peter and Andrew, James and John.

It was Peter's booming and not very peaceful voice He heard first, even before He saw the disciples walking along the road from town. They were loudly engaged in a vigorous discussion. James and John were on the receiving end of Peter's opinions, but they gave as well as they got. The rest were walking behind, discussing less vociferously among themselves, yet showing a visible disdain for what they were hearing from the three. Jesus sighed and stifled a laugh.

Just before recently returning to Capernaum, He and the three debating disciples had gone up on one of the nearby mountains. There Jesus was transfigured before them, shining like the sun in His glory. Moses and Elijah appeared with Him, and God Himself spoke to them: "This is My beloved Son, with whom I am well-pleased; listen to Him!" The three men's awe on the mountaintop, though, faded as quickly as they descended the hill, met the other disciples, and started discussing what it all meant. It seemed those debates were still going on as the disciples approached Jesus, who was now stand-ing and facing them, smiling as they arrived. Peter, without even a greeting for Jesus, blurted out impulsively, "Who then is greatest in the kingdom of heaven?" He obviously thought he already knew the answer.

The laugh that Jesus had stifled now burst out of Him as He moved forward to embrace Peter with a hearty hug, grab his shoul-ders, and meet the fisherman's flummoxed gaze with a broad smile. He looked at the other men's uncertain faces and then suddenly turned and called out to a young boy of about five years old, one of the children He had teased and laughed with earlier. The boy came, a bit sheepishly at first. He relaxed as Jesus smiled, took his hand, and led him into the midst of the disciples.

Jesus knelt down next to the boy, put His arm around him, and began to speak while looking at the child. "Truly I tell you, unless you change and become like little children, you will never enter the kingdom of heaven." He glanced at the boy's playmates, then looked up at the disciples, meeting each man's eyes. He spoke deliberately. "Therefore, whoever takes the lowly position of this child is the greatest in the kingdom of heaven. And whoever welcomes one such child in my name welcomes me." He paused to let that unexpected—and likely unsatisfying—answer to the question sink in before saying what He knew would raise their hackles even more. "If anyone causes one of these little ones—those who believe in me—to stumble, it would be better for them to have a large millstone hung around their neck and to be drowned in the depths of the sea."

Jesus stood up, gently tousled the boy's hair, and sent him back to his friends. He knew what His disciples were thinking now. This was not the answer they were hoping for. They wanted Him to name names, to declare which one of them would be His favorite in the coming Kingdom. But instead, He was telling them what they would have to do to *become* the greatest—they would have to change, become like this lowly child, and even honor children in the Master's name. Even worse, from their perspective, they would have to affirm the faith of children, as though a child's faith was just as valid as their own—a child whose faith meant nothing under Jewish law. Some of them had seen Him glorified, had seen Moses and Elijah and heard the voice of God. He knew what they were ultimately wondering: *Is He telling us our faith is deficient?* He knew they wouldn't grasp His words now, but eventually they would understand.

Jesus continued his teaching as evening encroached. Soon He and the disciples would leave Capernaum and travel to Judea, east of the Jordan, before going to Jerusalem for the last time. And yet James and John would continue to jockey for position in Jesus' Kingdom, Peter would ask Jesus what their reward would be for following Him, and the disciples would prevent parents from bringing their children to Jesus for a blessing, prompting a rebuke and a reminder from Jesus that "the kingdom of heaven belongs to such as these." And soon, the disciples would enter the final week of the Savior's life. He had told them the Cross was coming, but they didn't understand. As Jesus, the Messiah and the Son of God, would be cruelly stripped of His life, the disciples would be stripped of all their false expectations of greatness, thoughts of worldly reward, and hope for an earthly kingdom that would overthrow Rome. With clarified vision, they would finally come to understand what Jesus meant about His Kingdom—and the faith of a child.[1]

❧ ❧

Sometimes a story can reveal truth as well as a lesson, which we can see in the way Jesus skillfully used parables and illustrations throughout his ministry. The story about Jesus and His disciples in Capernaum is a first step toward thinking about strengthening your child's faith. As we move forward in the chapter, it will also be helpful to look more closely at what the Bible says—first about faith, and then specifically about a child's faith.

It's not my intention to do a comprehensive word study of biblical faith; instead, I want us to get a handle on biblical faith so we can better understand childhood faith. It's also not my concern to explore theological topics such as justification by faith or faith versus works, and I will touch only briefly on childhood conversion. Rather, I want to identify several practical expressions of faith that your child can understand and develop in order to interact with the life of God in your home.

What Is Faith?

Faith, at its simplest, is active belief. We tend to think of it first in terms of faith in God, whether in the Judeo-Christian God or gods of other religions, but we're all people of faith in many other ways too. We talk about "having faith" in people we trust, objects we use, sources of information we consult, expectations we have about life, and much more. The Greek words for "faith" and "belief" incorporate both sacred and secular aspects too. However, the New Testament writers added a new dimension to faith that, according to Dr. Larry Richards, "is never done in secular Greek"—the idea of faith "into." Richards describes the addition of the Greek preposition *eis* ("into") as "an invention of the early church that expresses the inmost secret of our faith" by portraying "a person committing himself or herself totally to the person of Jesus Christ, for our faith is *into* Jesus."[2]

Here's why that's important to lifegiving parenting: The faith that you need to strengthen in your children is not just a general belief in God or the spiritual realm; it's about Jesus and how He changes everything. Richards goes on to note that the object of faith in the New Testament is predominantly Jesus; only twelve verses mention God as the object.[3] Christian faith is Christocentric—it centers on the person of Jesus and our relationship with Him. Our faith is also cruciform, or shaped by the cross—it centers on the work of Jesus for us. Going back to how the church added the term *eis* to faith, it's not a pun to say that we should want our children to be "into" Jesus. We should want to strengthen their faith so they'll begin to believe that the Jesus they read about in the Bible is God—He became a man, died on the cross to deliver us from sin, and now rules His spiritual Kingdom here on earth from heaven. That is the gospel, and it is good news for your children as well as for you, their parents.

But even that kind of gospel-driven faith has many more nuanced biblical aspects. I can't cover them all here, but I do want to very briefly examine several facets of faith you can strengthen in your children. The stronger their childlike faith, the more they'll be able to experience the life of God, even in childhood. When Jesus tried to offer His message to His hometown of Nazareth, "He did not do many miracles there because of their unbelief" (see Matthew 13:53-58). A lack of faith in Jesus, or even a weak faith, can become a barrier to being able to recognize His life and work.

Your goal as a lifegiving parent is to make your home a little Capernaum, a place where Jesus is at home . . . where He lives and works because He finds faith there—faith in Him. And even more, it's a place where the faith of children—*your* children—is valued and honored in the ways Jesus described to His disciples, "for the kingdom of heaven belongs to such as these." Let's look at five facets, or qualities, of that kind of biblical faith: belief, trust, assurance, allegiance, and life.

Faith as Belief

Paul's letter to the Roman church is a practical exposition of Christian faith—who, what, why, and how to believe to be saved. In his magnum opus on the gospel of Christ, Paul mentions faith and believing over sixty times in sixteen chapters. His lead-off statement to his defense of the gospel asserts that it is "the power of God for salvation to everyone who believes," and that "in [the gospel] the righteousness of God is revealed from faith to faith [i.e., only by faith]; as it is written, 'But the righteous man shall live by faith'" (Romans 1:16-17). In other words, true life with God begins and ends with faith.

Later in the letter, Paul gets even more specific about the "word of faith" (10:8) that he is preaching, "that if you confess with your mouth Jesus as Lord, and believe in your heart that God raised Him from the dead, you will be saved; for with the heart a person believes, resulting in righteousness, and with the mouth he confesses, resulting in salvation" (vv. 9-10). Saving faith is both external and internal—it cannot be one without the other. Paul's point is that if people truly believe with their hearts, they will also confess (*homologeō*), or literally "speak the same," with their mouths. What begins with internal believing works its way out in external faith.

Strengthening the faith of your children begins with believing—getting beliefs about the gospel right in their hearts from the start. You have a brief but divinely designed window into your children's hearts during childhood, when they are predisposed by God's design to believe what you tell them about God, the gospel, and following Jesus. That doesn't mean pressuring them to say the words to the sinner's prayer (more on that later) but rather talking about what the gospel means to you, what you believe about Jesus, and how you are living by faith because of what you believe, all in ways that will let them see those things are real to you. You want your children to want what you believe to be what they also believe.

Faith as Trust

Trust is both a choice and an action. You can believe a mushroom is edible; you can pick it up out of the soil by faith; but you won't trust that it is edible until you put it in your mouth. The Old Testament expression of faith is predominantly trust, expressed well by a popular proverb: "Trust in the LORD with all your heart and do not lean on your own understanding" (Proverbs 3:5). It's hard to find a page in the Psalms that doesn't have some expression of trusting in the Lord, taking refuge in Him, asking Him for help, looking to Him with assurance, or many other variations on trust. These are just a few examples: "The LORD is my strength and my shield; my heart trusts in Him, and I am helped" (28:7); "When I am afraid, I will put my trust in You" (56:3); and "I will say to the LORD, 'My refuge and my fortress, my God, in whom I trust!'" (91:2).

Trust is, at its heart, confidence that God is going to be the kind of God He says He is and do what He promises to do. It is a characteristic of all those in the book of Hebrews' "Hall of Faith":

"Without faith it is impossible to please Him, for he who comes to God must believe that He is and that He is a rewarder of those who seek Him" (11:6). John was confident of God's faithfulness: "This is the confidence which we have before Him, that, if we ask anything according to His will, He hears us" (1 John 5:14). Jesus affirmed our confidence in Him: "Do not let your heart be troubled; believe in God, believe also in Me" (John 14:1).

Trust is what you do when faced with an "Is this God's will for my family?" kind of choice—such as questions about moving, finances, church, education, or illness. If you're walking by faith and not by sight, then you will seek wisdom from God's Word, pray about the matter, make a decision, and then step out in faith to trust God with it. What you decide by faith and place in God's hands is an act of trust. When your children see you trusting God, it tells them with more than just words that you believe that God exists, that He cares, and that He will reward your act of trusting faith.

Faith as Assurance

"Now faith is the assurance of things hoped for, the conviction of things not seen" (Hebrews 11:1). That familiar passage is another way of saying "we walk by faith, not by sight" (2 Corinthians 5:7). But you have to go back one verse in the Hebrews passage to get the whole picture: "We are not of those who shrink back to destruction [when our confidence is challenged], but of those who have faith to the preserving of the soul" (Hebrews 10:39). When things don't go as hoped, we still live by faith, with assurance that our hope is secure because of what Jesus has done (see Hebrews 12:1-3).

Faith that is assured says, "God is faithful and trustworthy and has promised to be with me, so I will continue to walk by faith with Him no matter what." When we pray and step out in faith, and the "no matter what" begins to matter, the faith of assurance will still say, like Job, "Though He slay me, I will hope in Him" (Job 13:15). Or like

Habakkuk, facing famine, "Yet I will exult in the LORD, I will rejoice in the God of my salvation" (Habakkuk 3:18). Or like James, Jesus' brother, as the new church faced persecution, "Consider it all joy, my brethren, when you encounter various trials, knowing that the testing [proving] of your faith produces endurance" (James 1:2-3).

As lifegiving parents, you need to show your children you believe that God doesn't go away when things don't go your way—He is still alive, still living in and through you, and still loving you just as much as He always has. Your children need to see you living with the faith-assurance of God's faithfulness and trustworthiness, that "no matter what" you may be facing as a family you will continue to walk by faith and not by sight. That's faith as assurance.

Faith as Allegiance

Faith as personal allegiance is deciding to stand by Jesus. Paul beautifully expresses his personal allegiance to Christ in his letter to the Galatians, one of his earliest epistles: "I have been crucified with Christ; and it is no longer I who live, but Christ lives in me; and the life which I now live in the flesh [body] I live by faith in the Son of God, who loved me and gave Himself up for me" (2:20). Paul is not just describing his salvation but declaring his allegiance to Christ. He tells the Colossians to similarly live in Christ, "having been firmly rooted and now being built up in Him and established in your faith" (Colossians 2:7).

But there is also allegiance to "the faith," the idea that we must "contend earnestly for the faith which was once for all handed down to the saints" (Jude 1:3). Paul encouraged the Philippian believers to conduct themselves "in a manner worthy of the gospel of Christ" so that they would be "standing firm in one spirit, with one mind striving together for the faith of the gospel" (Philippians 1:27). He encouraged the saints in Corinth to "be on the alert, stand firm in the faith, act like men, be strong" (1 Corinthians 16:13) and declared in his final epistle, "I have fought the good fight, I have finished the course, I have kept the faith" (2 Timothy 4:7).

Allegiance is loyalty. It is what will show your children that your family's beliefs are not fickle or temporary but firm and established. Like good citizens of the new Kingdom to which you belong, you are loyal both to your King (Jesus) and to His Kingdom. As a life-giving parent, when you affirm and rehearse your family's allegiance to everything "the faith" represents, that loyalty to Christ will give your children both a spiritual stability and a grand vision for life. When you remind them that your allegiance is to something much bigger than just your family, you are connecting them to the life of God that gives meaning to everything.

Faith as Life

Faith is the key that opens the door to life, and life is the ultimate end of faith. What begins with *belief* in Jesus in the heart is expressed through *trust* in Him by our choices and actions, sustained by confident *assurance* in His character, and established by loyal *allegiance* to Him and His Kingdom; and it will ultimately result in *life* in all its fullness. Jesus said, "I came that they may have life, and have it abundantly" (John 10:10), or over and above our expectations. John said, "And the testimony is this, that God has given us eternal life, and this life is in His Son. He who has the Son has the life; he who does not have the Son of God does not have the life" (1 John 5:11-12). Faith is the means to find both abundant life in the here and now and eternal life in the hereafter.

Perhaps the most powerful—and poetic—expression of faith as our source of God's life is by Peter in the preamble to his second letter. He opens by greeting his readers "who have received a faith of the same kind as ours, by the righteousness of our God and Savior, Jesus Christ" and reminding them that "His divine power has granted to us everything pertaining to life and godliness" (2 Peter 1:1-3). In other

STRENGTHENING YOUR CHILD'S FAITH   111

words, their faith is the entrance into life in God. What follows is a poetic description of how they "may become partakers of the divine nature" (v. 4). It begins with "applying all diligence, in your faith supply . . ." and then lists seven godly virtues that build one upon the other, ensuring that "the entrance into the eternal kingdom of our Lord and Savior Jesus Christ will be abundantly supplied to you" (see vv. 5-11). That abundant life in God's eternal Kingdom begins with faith.

This is the life that you bring into your home as a lifegiving parent in order to strengthen your children's faith. Giving your children a stronger faith is not just about having them memorize Scriptures, read Christian books, or do Bible lessons. It is ultimately about your showing them the abundant life of God through your own faith life and showing that you are diligent to grow in all the godly virtues that come out of your faith. None of us will ever exhibit all those virtues perfectly, but your children will see you making faith your priority, trusting God to transform your life, and depending on Him when you falter. It's not about having "arrived" but about walking daily with God. You can teach your children what Scripture says about faith and belief, but they will learn best about the reality of faith when it is lived out before their eyes in your life. That is lifegiving parenting.

What Is the Faith of a Child?

Now that we have a handle on what the Bible generally says about faith, we need to ask what it says about the faith of a child. When we teach our children about God, are we really strengthening their faith, or are we just doing the preliminary groundwork for a full expression of faith that will come when they are older?

Let's start by considering the narrative that opened this chapter, where Jesus made a striking statement about childhood faith that is easy to miss if you aren't looking for it. He was answering Peter's impulsive question about who would be the greatest in the Kingdom of Heaven. First, Jesus said that the greatest in the Kingdom would be the one who would willfully put himself at the same lowly level as a child. Second, He warned the disciples (with hyperbole) that anyone who caused one of these children "who believe in Me" (Matthew 18:6) to stumble might be better off dead. Keep in mind that in Jewish cultural hierarchy, no one was lower than children—they had no standing before the Jewish law. Yet Jesus elevated them to being a barometer of Kingdom greatness, and even more shockingly, He acknowledged the faith of a child as both valid and valuable.

The child Jesus brought before the disciples was a *paidion*, which means he was probably no more than seven years old. And yet Jesus says that the child is able to believe in Him, using the verb for faith (*pisteuō*) that is also used for adult belief. Jesus acknowledges the spirituality of children—they can believe in Him! He also indicates that adults can cause a young child to "stumble" (*skandalizō*) (v. 6), which can mean causing someone to sin or fall away (from faith), possibly by leading that person to distrust a trustworthy person. Causing a child to be tempted not to believe in Jesus is a scandal worthy of death. A child's immature faith is obviously not the same as an adult's mature faith, and yet Jesus commends the nascent faith of a child, both as a valid belief in Him and as devoid of pride and self-promotion.

Earlier, while pronouncing judgments on unrepentant cities, Jesus praised God because He had "hidden these things from the wise and learned, and revealed them to little children" (Matthew 11:25, NIV). Here Jesus uses the term *nēpios*, which refers to an infant. We won't speculate how spiritual truths are revealed to an infant; we simply note that Jesus says they are. Later, as Jesus arrives at the Temple after His triumphal entry into Jerusalem and older children are singing praises to Him, he has to remind indignant Jewish leaders about Psalm 8:2, that "out of the mouth of infants and nursing babies [God has] prepared praise for [Himself]" (see Matthew 21:15-16). So even in the Old Testament we see God affirming children's faith.

Finally, there's Timothy. In Paul's last epistle, he reminds his trusted protégé about his upbringing: "From infancy you have known the Holy Scriptures, which are able to make you wise for salvation through faith in Christ Jesus" (2 Timothy 3:15, NIV). Paul says that even when Timothy was a very small child (*brephos*), he was able somehow—presumably through his mother and grandmother (see 2 Timothy 1:5)—to know the Scriptures that would lead him to faith in Christ. The word *brephos* can actually refer to a child who is still in the womb. Again, I won't speculate on the how but will simply affirm that children, even perhaps still in the womb, are affected by our faith as lifegiving parents.

Here's the point: God sees a valid and even vibrant faith in children of all ages—in your children! As lifegiving parents, make it your commitment to look for that faith in your children, acknowledging and affirming it whenever you can. It probably won't sound like adult faith, and that's as it should be. It's an innocent and seedling kind of faith that should be watered, cultivated, and tended. It's possible you'll be tempted to correct its immature or misdirected expressions or, perhaps worse, to just ignore it; but resist either urge. Instead, engage your children's faith and draw it out. Give them room to grow, and help give their belief even more expression. Since you'll be following Jesus' teachings on children, there should be no better way to bring the life of God into your home.

Keeping Faith in the Family

To close out this chapter, I want to take you back to the five facets of faith we looked at above and explore very briefly how you can strengthen each of those aspects of your children's faith. Since faith is the key that opens the door to life in Christ, this is a critical heartbeat of lifegiving parenting. These suggestions are only a tiny first step on what will be a much longer journey of strengthening your children's faith, but what happens here can make the difference in giving them a strong start.

Strengthening Faith as Belief

"What if my child dies before asking Jesus into their heart?" That's a good question that has plagued many parents. In the limited space of this chapter, I'm not able to fully answer it and defend my views on childhood innocence and the mercy and grace of God (I do so at length in my book *Heartfelt Discipline*). However, I do want to discuss where that question often leads—to a misguided attempt to get a child to say "the sinner's prayer" (confessing sin, asking forgiveness, receiving Jesus as Savior) as early as possible. Unfortunately, it is too often done more to assuage a parent's fear than to awaken a child's faith.

The problem is that cajoling young children into repeating a prayer will not necessarily mean they have "saving faith." If children pray to please you rather than God, or because they feel pressured or coerced, then the prayer may sound sweet and innocent, but it is not likely a sinner's prayer of repentance or a true plea for mercy and forgiveness. The words by themselves do not save. Children will do things for their parents so Mom and Dad won't be angry or displeased with them, or even because they can see they will get affirmation from pleasing them.

That said, any signs of early faith should be recognized as genuine expressions of childlike faith in Jesus and in His presence in your life as a family. Always affirm faith in Jesus when you see or hear it. Even if your child prays a prayer of salvation, be careful not to turn it into an exaggerated celebration that could distort the perception of that event. Instead, say something like, "We're so happy that you want to believe in Jesus. We want to love Him as a family, and it pleases Jesus that now you believe in Him too." That kind of response will affirm both your child's developing faith and the life of God in your home. If it's a true prayer of salvation, then their new life with God will grow. However, if it is a prayer to please you, then you can still consider that expression an important stepping-stone of faith to affirm. In either case, your child is safe in God's grace and mercy. As a lifegiving parent, you are the key to strengthening their faith.

Strengthening Faith as Trust

Children are naturally trusting. They will readily be willing to trust God with a problem, whether it's theirs or their family's, if you are trusting God as a parent. They will trust God because they trust you. However, children can also be naturally fearful—they can become anxious about a problem if it challenges their expectations and experiences of life, especially if they see you being anxious. You are the key to converting a faith decision into a daily attitude of trusting God.

If you have a faith decision to make that can be shared with your children, plan a time to discuss the issue and pray about it as a family. Then come to a decision and step out in faith, believing God will help. That's the easy part. The hard part is for you, the lifegiving parent, to become a living example to your children of what it looks like to trust God with that decision every day after you pray.

In your family prayers, or just at a natural time during the day, remind your children about your faith decision and let them know how you're trusting God with it. Give them the opportunity to talk about their own trust, or their fears. Affirm your faith, God's faithfulness, and their faith, and then briefly pray about the decision. They'll grow stronger in faith.

Strengthening Faith as Assurance

Holding onto faith "no matter what" is a much harder concept for children, simply because they have not had enough life experience to know about God's faithfulness firsthand. When life becomes difficult, they have no history to draw from to strengthen their childish faith. You are the one they will look to for assurance. You are the one who will need to believe for them that God does not go away when life goes awry.

For instance, if there is an illness in your family, whether of a child or a parent, your children can become understandably confused, anxious, or fearful. That is normal and expected. In order to move to a place of trust and assurance, they will need to hear words of faith and assurance from you—meaningful Scriptures, your own expressions of assurance and hope, prayers for God's help, quotes and writings by spiritual writers, and affirmations of God's goodness, love, and mercy. Your assurance—that God is present and good no matter what happens or how your prayers are answered—will strengthen their faith.

Strengthening Faith as Allegiance

Children naturally want to be a part of something—your family, your church, a club, a team. That will make strengthening faith as allegiance to Jesus and His Kingdom easier, but it's not a given since the concept of being loyal to God is more abstract. In order to tap into your children's natural desires to belong, you'll need to find ways to express faith-allegiance as a family or to create a group of friends who can make the allegiance more of a concrete experience.

The concept of Kingdom is a wonderfully tangible idea that your child will naturally be able to imagine. Consider having a monthly Kingdom Night for your family when you imagine, reenact, or write out stories about being warriors for truth in God's Kingdom. Or start a Kingdom Kids Club with a few of your child's "good and godly" best friends. Plan for fun food, read-aloud stories, playacting, and club materials (names, crests, documents). This imagination cultivation (see chapter 9) is much more than just playtime. It is creating patterns of allegiance to strengthen your child's faith.

Strengthening Faith as Life

If you're living as a lifegiving parent, bringing the life of God into your home by following the patterns suggested in this book, then you will be strengthening your children's faith life. Jesus promised that He came to earth so that we would be able to have an abundant, beyond-all-our-expectations kind of life—not just in the hereafter but also in the here and now. That is what lifegiving parents represent to their children. And when your children come into contact with the real and living God who is present in your home, their faith will come alive. The more your children see the life of God in you through your faith, the stronger their faith will become.

⁂

Picture your own young child, a boy or a girl, standing in the midst of the twelve disciples. Jesus is kneeling down with His arm around your precious one, speaking these words as you look on: "If anyone causes one of these little ones—those who believe in me—to stumble, it would be better for them to have a large millstone hung around their neck and to be drowned in the depths of the sea" (Matthew 18:6, NIV).

Perhaps your ears are attuned to faith when you hear those words, "these little ones—those who believe in me." You know instinctively by faith that Jesus is holding up as an example your own child's belief in Him. You also know how messy, squirrelly, and random your child's faith can seem at times, and yet Jesus is affirming even that. He doesn't disclaim it or minimize it. He simply acknowledges it. And if it's good enough for Jesus, then how can it be any less for you?

But then you hear His words of warning. You know Jesus is using some oratorical hyperbole, and yet you get His message loud and clear—"Your children's faith is real and important to Me. Don't do anything that might turn their hearts away from Me. Seriously!" And you simply say silently to Jesus, "I'm on this, Lord. No millstone needed. Take it by faith."

Sally's Lifegiving Momoirs

When Nathan was a young child, he was captivated by stories about heroes. He spent hours in his own costumes, doing battle with swords and shields against imaginary villains. We realized that one of the ways we could encourage him spiritually was to speak to him about the heroic story of faith he would live someday.

One night we were reading and acting out the story of David and Goliath. Nathan, with his cape and sword, wanted to be David, because he knew that David was the hero of the story. Clay, of course, was the gigantic Goliath, pretending to taunt the armies of Israel as Nathan, on the third step of the stairs, was ready to be defiant and brave for God. Clay ad-libbed some taunts with his deep Goliath voice: "I defy you, men of Israel. Send out a man. Come and fight me!" And then, looking at Nathan, he bellowed, "Why, you're just a boy. Am I a dog that you come to me with sticks? Are you a coward?" To which Nathan straightened his back, raised his sword, and shouted boldly back in his four-year-old voice, "Yes, I am!" He wasn't sure what a coward was, but if he was the hero, he would be one with all his heart. We couldn't contain our laughter, but we quickly recovered and went on to make sure the young hero David could slay Goliath.

I look back on that night more than twenty years later and see more than just a fun family story. Even then, Nathan was putting hero stories into his heart. He would go on to inhabit other heroes in his childhood such as Audie Murphy, the World War II hero (he dressed up and gave a speech about him), Colonel William B. Travis of the Alamo (since we were in Texas at the time), and his favorite hero, Superman. He told me once, "I think Superman is like Jesus because he came to earth to save people who needed help. That's what I want to do with my life." All those hero stories were cultivating in him a heart of faith. They would come out much later in a Bible study about heroes he wrote for young men, and even in *Different*, the book we wrote together about his struggles growing up with OCD. Having a hero's heart of faith helped him to overcome many challenges and go on to write and make films about young men choosing to be faithful. Nathan's life is a reminder to me that nothing is wasted in a child's heart when it's about building faith. He's still Superman saving people.

Lifegiving ParenTips

Strengthen your own faith. We've said this before, but Moses got it right in the Shema 3,500 years ago: You can't impress on your children's hearts what is not first impressed on your own. In other words, you can't fill a well of faith in their hearts if you don't keep your own well faith-full. Your children are smart enough to know when you're dipping the bucket of your heart into a dry well—they know when there's nothing there to quench their spiritual thirst. So the first priority for strengthening your children's faith as a lifegiving parent is . . . to strengthen your own faith! Make room for a daily time of reading in the Word and praying. You might use a Bible-reading plan and keep a journal handy to record what you hear God saying, prayers for your family, and special Scriptures. Or you could find a good Scripture-based devotional to read and reflect on, such as *My Utmost for His Highest* or *Streams in the Desert*. Consider listening to podcasts by pastors and speakers who encourage you spiritually.

Tell your own stories. It's no secret that children love stories. But stories can be more than just entertainment for children; they can be formative influences on their minds, hearts, and spirits. We are so convinced of the power of story for children that we have a ministry initiative called Storyformed.com for parents wanting ideas for the best stories in literature. But the best stories are not only from printed books but also from the book of your own life. Tell your children your own life stories about your childhood, your parents and home life, your biggest adventures, your worst mistakes, your most regretted missed opportunities, your love story with your spouse, their birth stories, how you became a Christian, and how you've grown in faith. Of course, they will especially love any funny stories or "you won't believe this" stories. And if you're inclined, they will love any stories you make up about them as heroic and brave children in a faraway (or not) kingdom. For extra credit, record your stories as you tell them so your children can listen to them again later.

Read the living Word. It has always been our conviction that the real purpose of a family devotional time should be not just to learn the Bible but also to love it. Children can learn the Bible and not love it, but they can't love the Bible and not learn it. However, too many parents fail to understand they can inadvertently make the Word less lovable when they read it unlovingly. Hebrews 4:12 says, "The word of God is living and active." Literally, because the word of God is living, it is effective in our spiritual lives. God's Word is a living thing! However, too many parents can read the Bible as though it were a dead and ineffective textbook. That tells children that the Bible is boring and unimportant. To counter this, learn to read the Bible with dramatic expression, timing, and emphasis. Be aware of your speed—don't read too quickly or slowly, and vary the pace where it is needed. In Old Testament stories, do your best to give each character a voice and personality. Read the Bible as though it is alive—because it is. When you love God's Word, your children will, too, and it will cultivate hearts of faith.

Starting the Heartbeat of Parental Lifegiving

Strengthening your child's faith starts with believing that the very young can experience real belief. When you realize Jesus affirmed the faith of a small child, you can help your children grow in the belief, trust, assurance, allegiance, and life of their young but genuine faith.

CHAPTER 7

SHAPING YOUR CHILD'S WILL

All Scripture is inspired by God and is useful to teach us what is
true and to make us realize what is wrong in our lives. It corrects
us when we are wrong and teaches us to do what is right.

2 TIMOTHY 3:16, NLT

BOYS WILL BE BOYS, especially with toys. Big Brother is introverted and sensitive and very protective of his new toys. He doesn't want his younger brother playing with his new model fighter jet complete with swept-back wings, jet-engine noises, missiles that launch from the fuselage, and an action-figure pilot with an ejection seat and parachute. It's special and, in his mind, off limits to his little brother, who is extroverted and impulsive, even careless. He's also hard on toys, whether his own or his brother's. You know where this is going.

Big Brother puts his jet plane toy up high on the shelf when he leaves the room, thinking it will be out of reach and safe there. His little brother bounds into the room, sees the new toy, and can't help himself. He pulls a chair over, stands on it, and reaches up to get the jet. Just to look at it, of course, not to play with it. He makes a couple of fly-by motions, shoots a missile, and then begins to lose his balance on the chair. He grabs the wall to steady himself but . . .

drops the jet. It crash-lands on the bedroom floor. Actually, it just lands with a crash, with various pieces and parts strewn around it, a missile gone missing, and a once-straight tail antenna now bent.

His big brother comes back into the room, sees his prized new jet toy on the floor, and loses his typically cool demeanor. He yells at his brother about being careless, wrong, and several other choice adjectives. His little brother offers an unconvincing, dispassionate "Sorry," then tries to blame the situation on his big brother for leaving the jet out where he could see it in the first place. It wasn't fair that his brother should get such a good toy, and it wasn't his fault that it broke (he offers no defense for that spurious claim but puts it forward with full conviction). The confrontation keeps deteriorating, and they both end up yelling at each other.

Mother, hearing the commotion, runs to the playroom to enter the fray. She quickly sizes up the situation, is sympathetic with her older son, scolds her younger son and makes him apologize, asks the older brother to forgive his younger brother, and makes them hug and be friends. Normally that's where this kind of boy battle typically ends, with an unsatisfying cease-fire, but this mom takes the opportunity to step up to another level of training. Mom sits the boys down on a bed to talk about their "Family Ways" and which ones might help them learn something in this situation. She says they won't be doing anything else until they can both name whatever Family Ways apply.

Though still visibly perturbed, the responsibility-oriented older boy starts by reciting one of the Ways. "We love each other, treating others with kindness, gentleness, and respect." He waits a few seconds, then adds another. "We choose to be peacemakers, even when we feel like arguing." He adds, "I guess I shouldn't have reacted and gotten so mad." Mom thanks him, acknowledging that she understands why he would be so upset but noting that his attitude now is admirable. She also gently encourages him to think about another of the Ways: "We are generous with what we have, sharing freely with others."

Mother looks at her younger son and waits. He is not so forthcoming and hems and haws. Finally he remembers and reluctantly recites a Way. "We are content with what we have, not coveting what others have." Mother nods and prompts another one by asking him about his self-control. He rolls his eyes and blurts out in a rush of words, "We exercise self-control at all times and in every kind of situation." Mother smiles and then adds one of her own: "We always tell the truth and do not practice deceitfulness of any kind." The younger boy frowns and hangs his head. Busted.

Mother hugs the two brothers, has them pray with each other, and then says they may go do other things now. Before they leave, though, she reminds them of one other Way: "We forgive one another, covering an offense with love when wronged or hurt." As she leaves the room, she sees Big Brother showing his little brother how the ejection seat works and the younger boy getting excited about finding the errant missile in a pile of his toy soldiers. She would have made them look up and read the Scripture verse attached to each of the Family Ways they identified, but since the intervention and training have gone so well, she decides it isn't needed. Boy battle number 2,379 resolved.

⋙ ⋘

That was a composite, totally fictionalized illustration, and one that, while certainly idealistic, is not completely unrealistic. However, the "Family Ways" are real—all twenty-four of them. We used them in our family from 1994, when I wrote them, until the late 2000s, when our youngest was in her early teens. There are four Ways in each of six areas of family life—authorities, relationships, possessions, work, attitudes, and choices—and each Way includes a key Scripture verse as well as a character quality and definition. Those twenty-four Family Ways were our first lifegiving parenting tool, and they became our primary family resource for shaping our children's wills. (See "Growing Your Child's Values" on pages 217–19 for the full list of "Our 24 Family Ways.")

Our Family Ways were conceived and written when we lived in Nashville, Tennessee, and our first three children were all under eight. Other workbooks available at the time offered "House Rules" lists, but they were just that . . . rules. Do this, don't do that, pick it up, turn it off. What I wanted for my children was a resource for influencing and shaping their wills based on biblical values. And rather than rules, I wanted ways, like God's way of life. I wanted a resource that would help me impart not just godly wisdom but also actual language for biblical family values and Christian character. When I wasn't able to find such a resource, I determined to create my own. I like to think that "Our 24 Family Ways" gives new meaning to the old saying, "Where there's a will, there's a way."

All parents know their children's wills exist from the moment their precious babies let out that first defiant "No!" As children get older, their developing wills get expressed in a myriad of choices— deciding which food to eat and whether to obey Mom and Dad, tell the truth, do the right thing, love others, ad infinitum. In essence, those developing wills are what ultimately determine who they become. The defining paths our children choose in adulthood begin with how their wills are trained and shaped in childhood. Children who are spoiled, coddled, and always allowed to have their own way will likely grow up with a self-justifying and selfish sense of entitlement. Children who are controlled, raised harshly, and never allowed any grace or freedom will likely grow up resentful, insecure, and angry. Children who are loved, directed, and given freedom to be who they are will likely grow up confident, secure, and loving.

Our children, like all humans, have many desires, drives, intentions, and loves that are neutral in and of themselves but can become good or bad depending on how we shape their wills and what they will to choose and pursue. It's all the work of what Scripture calls the soul, the inner person of the heart that is the locus of the mind, emotions, and will. Those three qualities of the soul all work together in the act of making choices, and yet the will alone translates thoughts and feelings into decisions. The will reveals who you are by what you choose and do.

And yes, sin is at work in your children's spirits, but not yet in the sense of willfully rebelling against God. There will come a time when they'll understand that their sin separates them from God, they'll turn to Jesus as their Savior, and the Spirit will give them a new nature in Christ that will break the power of sin over their souls. In most of childhood, though, shaping your children's wills is more about winning the tug-of-war between their immature, undeveloped selves and your mature parental influence. It's about your shaping and preparing their wills for the time when they will need to choose Jesus over self and teaching them the blessings and benefits of obedience to God's will.

Paul makes it easy on parents, though, by teaching them, and their children, that childhood obedience to God's will really comes down to obeying and honoring their parents with both actions and attitudes—"Children, be obedient to your parents in all things, for this is well-pleasing to the Lord" (Colossians 3:20) and "Children, obey your parents in the Lord, for this is right" (Ephesians 6:1). It's simply a matter, Paul says, of honoring the fifth commandment: "Honor your father and mother" (v. 2). So shaping your children's wills is influencing them, through your loving relationship with them, to honor you. Would that it were that simple.

Some parents can fall into a one-sided pattern of demanding obedience but not honor. In other words, you can make your children stop a wrong or unwanted behavior ("Stop whining right now!") but then ignore the dishonor in their hearts (pouting, sulking, anger).

That certainly isn't ideal for shaping your children's wills, but neither is making every situation a "me, parent . . . you, child" confrontation. Part of shaping and influencing your children's wills effectively means learning to be sensitive to issues of age, personality, and circumstances, not expecting the same kind of obedience from a five-year-old that you would from a ten-year-old, or not demanding perfect obedience when your children are tired or overstimulated. If obedience is your children learning to show their love for God (see John 14:15), then your job is not just to control your children but also to love them for God—to show them in some way what God's love is like—and help them love God better.

It's important to understand that you can't really control your children's wills. They can be shaped and molded, but they are not things you can train and control as you would the family dog. Sure, you may be able to "control" your children's behavior to some degree, usually through fear of punishment, but that control will not necessarily influence and shape their hearts, which control their wills. Just because you can, by whatever means, make your children obey your will, that does not mean they are obeying from their hearts. That's why this chapter is about shaping the will, not just training or controlling it. For this heartbeat of lifegiving parenting, I'm more concerned about helping you understand how to shape and mold your children's wills to respond to your parental influence, which is about relationship, than I am about helping you control their behavior, although we'll look briefly at that, too.

Jesus was a Jewish rabbi, which simply means "teacher" (see John 1:38). A Jewish adage He quotes in a parable goes right to the heart of what it means to shape your children's wills. Jesus said, "A pupil [or learner] is not above his teacher; but everyone, after he has been fully trained [or prepared], will be like his teacher" (Luke 6:40). The word translated "trained" (*katartizō*) here means to be prepared. It also shows up in a prayer in the letter to the Hebrews, calling on God to equip (or prepare) them "in every good thing to do His will" (13:21). Shaping your children's wills to respond to you and to God is preparing them to be ready to respond to God to "do His will," both by accepting Jesus as their Savior and by obeying Him as their Lord.

For a lifegiving parent, shaping your children's wills is about influencing their hearts to want to do the will of God. You don't shape your children's wills just so they'll be good decision makers; you shape their wills so they will be prepared to do God's will when it is clearly known and act on other biblical principles when it is not. It's never just an impersonal or logical process; it's about a personal and spiritual relationship with the Lord. That's why shaping your children's wills is a heartbeat of lifegiving parenting—you are connecting them with the living God.

I use the word *shaping* rather than *training* because shaping speaks more to a two-way relational influence, while training suggests one-way, nonrelational control. The former is more grace driven, the latter more law driven. The difference between law and grace will have a defining impact on how your child grows up thinking about and doing God's will.

Shaping Your Child's Will with Grace and Truth

John reminds us that "the Law was given through Moses; grace and truth were realized through Jesus Christ" (John 1:17). Parenting involves this tension between the Law and the grace and truth of Christ. Immature children are going to be inconsistent at best in responding to your influence and training. That's the reality of the human will and the sin nature. However, the unfortunate and too-typical parental response to children's errant wills is to "lay down the law" with serious and sometimes painful consequences. That kind of negative training results in fear or anger. You can become a parental adversary, looking for every wrong behavior to correct and punish (law), rather than a parental advocate, looking for good behavior to affirm and reward (grace). You may be able to train your children to fear doing the wrong thing, but that does not mean you've trained them to love doing the right thing.

God's grace is a positive, lifegiving force in your life and your child's; law is a negative, punitive one: "Sin shall not be master over you, for you are not under law but under grace" (Romans 6:14). Law is an external standard of rules and regulations we must keep to try to please God. Grace, though, is an internal standard of truth and freedom that we live by through the power of the Holy Spirit. "If you are led by the Spirit, you are not under the Law" (Galatians 5:18). If you want to shape your child's will in a Christlike way, then let your influence be characterized by His grace and by God's Holy Spirit.

This leads to an important caveat: Grace is not parental license to overlook or indulge wrong behavior. Paul makes that clear: "The grace of God has appeared that offers salvation to all people. It teaches us to say 'No' to ungodliness and worldly passions, and to live self-controlled, upright and godly lives in this present age" (Titus 2:11-12, NIV). Grace is not permission to be passive as a parent; rather, it's participation in an active force that continually "teaches us" to say no to anything that is not God and yes to everything that is. That's the kind of grace you want your children to know—grace to do right and to refrain from doing wrong.

What does this kind of grace look like? Let me suggest one Scripture for all parents to keep in mind: "Let no unwholesome word proceed from your mouth, but only such a word as is good for edification according to the need of the moment, so that it will give grace to those who hear" (Ephesians 4:29). An "unwholesome word" means not only a bad or filthy word but also one that is of poor quality, worn out, and no longer fit for use—such as legalistic words of law, the kind that point out only how far our children are from pleasing God. Instead, our words should be the kind that edify, or build up, others according to their needs and that are spoken intentionally to "give grace." In our years of parenting ministry, we've observed that parents who are harsh, critical, and legalistic close off and lose their children's hearts. But those who are kind, loving, and gracious open and win their children's hearts. To shape your children's wills, first open their hearts with grace that will build them up—words of love, kindness, mercy, respect, encouragement, and hope.

Grace has power to shape your child's will, but you need both grace and truth. Grace takes you to the heart of God; truth takes you to the mind of God. You can't know truth without God's grace, and you can't understand grace without God's truth. However, in training your child's will, it's easy to stop at either the heart (grace) or the mind (truth), thinking enough has been done. For instance, if you're correcting a child's lie, you might hear her express a sincere regret for her sin and stop there (grace); or you might hear her recite a key Bible verse and stop there (truth). To fully engage the will, though, your child needs to hear both grace and truth—experiencing the forgiveness that comes through grace and understanding the godly standards of behavior that come through truth.

Paul told his protégé Timothy, "Every scripture is inspired by God and useful for teaching, for reproof, for correction, and for training in righteousness, that the person dedicated to God may be capable and equipped for every good work" (2 Timothy 3:16-17, NET©). He had just reminded Timothy of the power that Scripture had wielded in his childhood (v. 15), which led Paul to this statement. Because of that context, there are few better passages about shaping your children's wills with truth. Paul's words reveal a process: "teaching" explains the standard, "reproof" stops a sin, "correction" restores the sinner, "training in righteousness" instructs him or her how to move forward, and it all results in making followers of God "capable and equipped" for whatever they do. The term for "training" here is *paideia,* which often refers to the instruction of children in both their minds and their morals. This is what Scripture does when you use it for shaping your children's wills.

Teaching truth from God involves more than getting information about the Bible into your children's minds. In our years of teaching about teaching children, one reality is consistent—all children love stories. You know this intuitively from how your children respond to and remember stories, and from how Jesus used parables and stories as an effective teaching tool. I don't want to minimize all that the Bible teaches about life and God that you and your children simply need to know. However, even those parts of Scripture are found within larger stories of history, events, context, and relationships, all of which can help bring the harder truths of Scripture alive with story for your children. Find the story to tell about the truth you want your children to know and remember, and let the story tell the truth.

But there's more to a well-shaped will than what grace and truth alone can create. The very nature of the will is choice and action, which lead to the need for diligence.

Shaping Your Child's Will for Diligence

Solomon had enough children that he could say from experience, "Even a young man is known by his actions, whether his activity is pure and whether it is right" (Proverbs 20:11, NET©). Though he speaks of a young man, the principle is certainly true of children, too—the way children act reveals their character. And one of the most telling character qualities in children is diligence—responding positively to parental influence and doing without delay what needs to be done. This is not primarily about obedience but about willing-ness. The writer of Hebrews affirms his readers' diligence in their work, love, and ministry for God, contrasting it with being "sluggish" (6:11-12). Sluggish children, in the same way, are slow, resistant, and negative. Diligence is a barometer that shows how effectively you are shaping your children's wills.

Some children, based on personality differences, will be more naturally diligent than others, but diligence is a nonnegotiable for shaping your children's wills. The lack of it, or the persistence of a "sluggish" nature, is a character deficiency that needs to be overcome if you hope to train your children's wills to want to do the will of God. Above all, your children need to see what diligence looks like from your model—they will not be motivated to become what they do not see you wanting to become. They need to see you being quick to respond when the Holy Spirit leads you to do something, and diligent to correct a fault or do what is right when convicted.

Diligence is a habit—the more it is practiced, the more it becomes a part of your children's natures. Define some projects for them and then patiently encourage diligence to accomplish the tasks, working alongside if that helps. The more you can create patterns of diligence, the more it will become a habit, regardless of personality.

Occasional positive incentives can help to encourage diligence. A reward should not be expected for every task and should not be offered too often, but offering reasonable rewards for children who diligently accomplish certain projects or establish new habits can motivate less naturally diligent children to try harder. Remember that diligence is an internal matter of character—it is a spiritual issue because someone who is not diligent will not be quick to obey God. So pray regularly about your children's willingness to be diligent and let them know you're asking God to help them.

Endurance, or "stick-to-itiveness," is also part of diligence. Your children will at times want to quit something because it's too hard, but James says this: "Consider it all joy, my brethren, when you encounter various trials, knowing that the testing of your faith produces endurance" (James 1:2-3). In other words, trials should not be seen as only negative; they also serve as positive ways to test faith and show that it is genuine. Of course you will try to protect your children from significant trials, but they can still learn endurance. That may come through an extended exercise of diligence to complete a school, club, or home project, or it may be a faith or character goal of some kind (physical, educational, financial, etc.) that will require them to persevere over a long time to reach it. It could be learning a new skill, memorizing large portions of Scripture, writing a book, or any number of challenging tasks that will require your children to exercise endurance. Endurance can be learned.

Diligence and endurance are part of a well-shaped will because they increase our ability to act when we are asked to. However, the will still needs to make the right choices. Even if parents communicate with grace and truth and shape their children's wills to include diligence and endurance, they will still need to use corrective discipline. Discipline is a critical part of shaping the will.

Shaping Your Child's Will with Discipline

When you hear the words "childhood discipline," you probably think immediately of punishment since we've been conditioned to associate discipline with consequences for disobedience. You might also think about a range of hands-on, hands-off, and hands-around methods of discipline that you've read about or heard taught. The purpose of this chapter is to help you think about how to influence and shape your children's wills, not how to discipline or train your children. And yet childhood discipline is about the will, so it is by default part of your will-shaping relationship with your children.

In my book *Heartfelt Discipline*, I suggest what I believe is the oldest and most biblical concept of childhood discipline—God's path of life. I show that biblical discipline is more than just the punishment that we typically associate with it; it's also about keeping children on God's path by providing *direction* (showing your children how to stay on the path of life), *correction* (bringing them back when they stray off the path), and *protection* (guarding them against temptations that could draw them off the path).[1] This more nuanced view of biblical discipline is also a more natural and holistic approach to shaping the will of your children. It focuses on the same relational picture of parents and children walking together on God's path of life that we looked at in chapter 4 during our discussion about guarding your children's hearts.

Discipline is about reaching your children's hearts, which include their wills. In the more than nine hundred references to "heart" in Scripture, the meaning is consistent—the heart is who you are, the "inner person" of spirit, mind, emotion, and will. Jesus said that people speak from the overflow of whatever is in their hearts, whether good or evil (see Luke 6:45). Your children are like PowerPoint presentations of whatever is directing their hearts. Biblical discipline is not just about correction but also direction—filling your children's hearts with as much good as you can and then influencing and shaping their wills to choose the PowerPoint slides of behavior that will please God.

I'll suggest three aspects of corrective discipline: spiritual discipline, verbal discipline, and behavioral discipline.

Spiritual discipline. This is not generally recognized as an actual disciplinary method, and yet it is arguably the heart of true biblical discipline. As parents, our first impulse is often to think about which proven method will achieve the results we want, but what we should think about first is trusting God to work in our children's hearts. Shaping the wills, or the hearts, of our children by discipline must begin as a spiritual act. Before we turn to methods, we must turn to God to ask Him to be involved in the process. The active part of spiritual discipline is the grace of God that we touched on earlier. But to take it another step, it's the life of God flowing into your family through channels of grace: God's Word, prayer, and fellowship.

First, turn to the Word with your children for guidance that is "able to judge the thoughts and intentions of the heart" (Hebrews 4:12). Have them memorize instructive Scriptures and Bible promises, and talk about them together. Second, pray to God for and with your children throughout the day. Pray for their hearts to be soft and responsive, and that God would bring Scriptures to their minds. Pray Scripture with them, letting the words of God be your words to God (for example, use the words of Psalm 25 or other psalms as a basis for prayer). Sally is a pray-now mother who would pour grace into our children many times each day by stopping to pray with them about anything and everything. Finally, fellowship with other Christians who will be models for your children. Let them see and hear as you "bear one another's burdens" (Galatians 6:2), "spur one another on toward love and good deeds" (Hebrews 10:24, NIV), and even confess weakness and the need for God's forgiveness.

This may not seem like discipline in the way we've been trained to think about it. But leading the way through Scripture, prayer, and fellowship is a sure way to shape our children's wills, showing them what it means to be connected with God, to respond to Him, and to let Him and His people influence our choices. When you start with the spiritual hearts of your children, you are letting them know that discipline is not just about them doing what you want them to do but is also about what God wants them to do.

Verbal discipline. Verbal discipline comes naturally to all parents; biblical verbal discipline only comes supernaturally. The latter requires more than just our ability to say "No!" or "Stop that!" to our children; it requires us to know the Scriptures, be able to recall them, and discern how to apply them for all aspects of discipline—but especially for corrective discipline. When we use the Word of God in our verbal discipline, we affirm to our children that we are their earthly authority and, even more important, that God is their ultimate authority. For instance, if children lie about their siblings, you can remind them of God's ninth commandment to "not bear false witness" (Exodus 20:16). Or if they are being unkind, read 1 Corinthians 13:4: "Love is patient, love is kind. . . ." If you don't know a Scripture, you can simply say, "Let's see what God says" and use a concordance to look up some passages together.

Christlike love is critical to effective verbal discipline. When we're correcting our children's wrongdoings, we can think about how Jesus would speak—gently but authoritatively; lovingly but truthfully; graciously but firmly. Our words should be characterized by the fruit of the Spirit and be loving, joyful, peaceful, patient, kind, good, faithful, gentle, and self-controlled (see Galatians 5:22-23). Strictness, harshness, anger, guilt, and legalism will not change our children's hearts or shape their wills for the good, and in fact can close their hearts to us. Gentleness keeps verbal discipline in the realm of grace, where children learn to obey from the heart for the right reasons—to please God and their parents. As all parents have experienced, we don't always get this right and can be harsh or legalistic despite our best intentions. Children are resilient, though, so simply acknowledging your parental shortcomings will be enough to put the matter back on the right track. Whatever the discipline issue may be, ask the Holy Spirit to help you be like Jesus to your children.

Also keep these guidelines in mind when you discipline verbally with the Word: *Speak the truth in love* (be the spirit of Jesus to your children); *assume your biblical authority* (speak with confidence); *apply God's Word* (to teach, reprove, correct, and train in righteousness; see 2 Timothy 3:16-17); *express a positive message* (let your children know you see their goodness, heart, and potential); and *seek a biblical response* (confession, forgiveness, repentance, conviction, godly sorrow). Be like Paul, "exhorting and encouraging and imploring" your children with the Word to walk in a way that will be pleasing to God (1 Thessalonians 2:11-12).

Behavioral discipline. The purpose of behavioral discipline is always the same—to make your children accountable for their own actions and choices. It could be called the if-then school of corrective discipline ("If you do that, then this will happen"), and it even has its own book in the Bible—Proverbs, which is all about making choices between wisdom and foolishness. In essence, behavioral discipline is shaping the wills of your children—helping them learn to control their impulses and desires. It is typically used to discourage wrongdoing or foolish behavior (see Galatians 6:7-8), but it can also be used as an incentive for "rightdoing."

The key to behavioral discipline is consequences, which even very young children can understand: "If you don't stop whining, Mommy won't listen to you." "If you leave your toys outside, we'll have to put them away for a week." The idea of consequences is to help your children learn to take responsibility for their own behaviors. There are two common forms of behavioral discipline: The first is *natural consequences*, which follows general foolishness and wrongdoing when parents and children have not previously agreed about a behavior. For instance, imagine a child being foolishly careless and breaking a new toy. The natural consequence will be disappointment, from which the child will learn to be more careful. The second is *logical consequences*. This follows specific wrongdoing when parents and children have previously agreed about certain behaviors. For instance, unkind words to a sibling might result in writing out an agreed-upon Scripture passage multiple times. Uncompleted chores might result in additional agreed-upon chores being assigned. Either way, the effect is that the consequence was not randomly imposed by you but was chosen by the child. Whichever the consequence, the shaping of your children's wills helps them take responsibility for their decisions.

❧　☙

Shaping your children's wills to want to obey God is one of the most challenging tasks you will encounter as a lifegiving parent. The fruit of your influence will be in direct proportion to the amount of time you can invest engaging in your children's lives physically, mentally, emotionally, and spiritually. It will be one of your most demanding responsibilities as a parent and yet one with arguably the greatest rewards. Who your children become as adults will, in many ways, be determined by how you influence and shape their wills now as children—they will become products of the choices they make in childhood and youth, whether good or bad, on your watch. God's path of life is all about choices, and you're shaping your children's wills to choose to stay on that path.

There is a paradox about shaping your children's wills that is true for every Christian parent. You're faithfully influencing your children to have a confident, firm will so they will be able to resist the world and follow God's will, and yet you're also strengthening their free will, which can choose to resist God's will in favor of their own. For Christians, free will becomes a paradox of faith—you're either a servant of sin or a servant of Christ, but you're never truly free. As Bob Dylan puts it, "It may be the devil or it may be the Lord, but you're gonna have to serve somebody."[2]

That's why it's never enough to focus only on your children's wills. Too many models of childhood discipline insist on the misguided concept of "immediate, complete, joyful" obedience as the only biblical standard for children's wills. Some believe that children's wills are the keys to their souls and must be broken and controlled lest the children be lost. I contend that the other lifegiving heartbeats— spirit, heart, mind, faith, character, imagination—are no less necessary for biblically shaping your child's will. Your child is a whole, complex, and wonderfully made person, not just a will.

No one alive ever had a more perfectly obedient will than Jesus. But even though He had a human nature and will, He chose to submit His will to that of His heavenly Father. That's why He could say, "I have come down from heaven, *not to do My own will*, but the will of Him who sent Me" (John 6:38, emphasis added). He had His own will, but He chose to do the Father's will. It's also what made

His struggle in Gethsemane real when He prayed, "Father, if You are willing, remove this cup from Me; *yet not My will*, but Yours be done" (Luke 22:42, emphasis added). Jesus expressed the same struggles with doing God's will that we would have, but He gave us an example of submitting to God's will even when it is difficult.

When you tell your children you're helping them to become more like Jesus, be sure they understand that includes their wills becoming like His. They can learn from Jesus how to discern the difference between "my will" and God's will, and how to submit to what God desires them to do, be, believe, and become. They can pray, like King David, "Teach me the way in which I should walk. . . . Teach me to do Your will, for You are my God" (Psalm 143:8, 10). When you purposely determine to shape your children's wills for Christ, you are bringing them fully into the life of God. He wants them to do His will, and He will do whatever He can to help them do it. He has even given your children faithful, lifegiving parents to shape their wills for Him.

Sally's Lifegiving Momoirs

When Joy was twelve years old, one of my friends desperately needed someone to help her with the little children at the Mom's Day Out program at a church in our area. I asked Joy if she would consider being the assistant, and she willingly agreed. She was always an especially positive and willing child. When she got to the program, she found out she would be helping with sixteen toddlers. You can imagine what all that entailed! She would come home and tell me stories of keeping the children entertained, clean, and under control, even though they, and sometimes even the moms she would interact with, were not self-controlled. It was much more than she had anticipated she would be called on to do, but she took it on and handled it with pluck and a good spirit. In fact, she told me that she had decided she wanted to be one of the program's best workers.

Joy is very strong-willed in the best way, and even as a young girl she was self-motivated to accomplish whatever she decided in her heart was right and she had set her mind to do. So for this job, she planned what toys and special activities to bring so she could be more effective with the toddlers; she knew each one's name, personality, and likes, and she threw herself into the job to do it as best as she could. The women in charge of the program had nothing but praise for her. The second year, they felt comfortable putting her, with an assistant, in charge of the toddlers and giving her a raise, because she was so diligent and capable and had earned their trust.

Joy worked there three years and put away a very nice nest egg of money for when she would later go to Biola University at seventeen (which is another story of her diligence and will). Looking back, I think Joy's time of working in what others might see as a rather difficult and thankless job not only strengthened her will but also created in her a sense of the value of being diligent. Recently, Joy and I went to one of our favorite coffeehouses while she was home for a break. With so many things happening in her life that required her to choose to keep going, she let me know she was grateful for learning that quality in her childhood and teens. She admitted it was partly her personality, but it was the training at home and the opportunities we provided that shaped her will and focused it.

Lifegiving ParenTips

Where there's a will. There are so many areas in which to shape children's wills that it can become overwhelming just trying to identify which are most important. That's part of what prompted me to write "Our 24 Family Ways" for training our children. (For a list of all 24 Ways, see "Growing Your Child's Values" on pages 217–19.) The six categories I used to organize the Ways—authorities, relationships, possessions, work, attitudes, choices—limited the scope of the Ways and made shaping the will seem more doable. If we wanted to focus on chores, for example, first we would select one of the four Ways about work, such as "We are diligent to complete a task promptly and thoroughly when asked." Then we would assign some new responsibilities to use as a test. We would make sure the children had memorized the Way, and then we would use it to affirm when they chose to be responsible and to confront when they did not. We would not use the Way to make them feel guilty but rather to let them assess their own progress and then encourage them to do better. The Way helped to neutralize the confrontational part of training the will. Whether or not you find the Ways useful, consider how you can create your own statements of biblical principles to use in developing character in your children.

Not my will but yours. Children are naturally self-concerned, so training them to a standard of "not my will" goes against their natural grain. The default response for most children will typically be their own desires, even though children express that differently. Extroverted and assertive children will be more verbal about wanting what they want; introverted and compliant children will keep what they really want more internal, but it's still there. One way to help change a pattern of self-will is to provide an example in your own life. It can be as simple as giving up part of a Saturday to help a widow in your church with her yard or to take an elderly friend out for a meal. Ask your children to join you in the act of service, and challenge them to think of anything they can do to make the time more special for the other person.

Give them the task of ensuring that the idea happens, and be sure to give them credit for it when you can. It's just a small thing, but it's one step toward loving others by giving up personal desires and expectations.

Tools for will-shaping. You need good tools for building things, whether it's a shed or children. Keep your child-training toolbox filled with tools you can pull out as needed. We've already talked about *Our 24 Family Ways* as a tool for creating language for training. Knowing your children's personality types is another specialty tool that will enable you to fine-tune your parental influence. The "Knowing Your Child's Personality" section in the back of this book, along with the material in chapter 8, can help you identify whether your children are Doers, Helpers, Movers, or Shapers and understand how each type relates to life differently. You might also compile a file of stories from your life about times when you had to set aside what you wanted in order to follow God. You can share these with your children at appropriate times when shaping their wills. Finally, have charts on hand, physically or digitally, that you can use to help your children track their progress toward being diligent and making wise choices. Rewards for those goals, when fitting, can be good incentives for training.

Starting the Heartbeat of Parental Lifegiving

Shaping your child's will starts with your will and God's. From the first defiant "No!" it is the challenge of Christian parenting to train your child's will through grace and truth, diligence, and discipline to honor and obey you and God.

CHAPTER 8

CULTIVATING YOUR CHILD'S CHARACTER

The seed in the good soil, these are the ones who have heard the word in an honest and good heart, and hold it fast, and bear fruit with perseverance.

LUKE 8:15

As SALLY HAS OFTEN TOLD parents when she speaks, a garden does not become beautiful by accident. You don't just throw a handful of seeds into the air and hope a lovely and fruitful garden will appear. In fact, the presence of a tended garden with rich soil, hoed rows, and healthy plants is undeniable evidence of the planning, work, and cultivation that went into making that raw patch of earth into a garden. And as Sally always goes on to say, that is true for parenting, too. If we want our "gardens"—our children—to be healthy and fruitful, with godly character, it's going to take some cultivation.

Jesus taught the same thing; you know this teaching as the parable of the Sower. It's all about cultivating good heart-soil, and though we don't always grasp Jesus' application to children in the parable, it's there and can change the way we think about child raising. The Sower is one of only six parables recorded in all three synoptic

Gospels—Matthew, Mark, and Luke. While there is little variation between the three Sower accounts, I'll use Luke's version (Luke 8:4-18) because it includes an important insight not recorded in the other two that speaks directly to cultivating character in your children. As we move through Luke's account of Jesus telling and explaining the parable, I'll include occasional details from the other Gospels.

Jesus is "proclaiming and preaching the kingdom of God" (8:1) along the Sea of Galilee with His twelve disciples. Many people coming from the cities to hear Him have walked through both wild and cultivated fields to get there. When they gather to hear Him teach, Luke notes that He speaks to them "by way of a parable" (v. 4) about a man who went out to sow. Jesus tells them that some of the Sower's seed fell beside the road and then was trampled underfoot and eaten by birds. Other seed fell on rocky soil, grew up, found no moisture, and withered away. Still other seed fell among the thorns, which choked out the seed as it grew. But other seed "fell into the good soil, and grew up, and produced a crop a hundred times as great" (v. 8).

When He finishes His brief Sower story, Jesus leaves it to the crowds to wrestle with the meaning of the parable. His disciples, though, want to know why He teaches with parables and what this one means. Jesus tells them that the "mysteries [or secrets] of the kingdom of God" have not been granted to all the people but revealed only to His followers (v. 10). However, He rebukes them for being so dense about something they should already know: "Don't you understand this parable? How then will you understand any parable?" (Mark 4:13, NIV). Then Jesus begins to explain the story to His disciples.

He begins with the seed. "The seed is the word of God" (Luke 8:11), He says, not meaning just the Old Testament Scriptures in this case but more specifically the seed of the gospel of the Kingdom of Heaven, a new word from God. The Sower represents anyone who understands the message of the Good News that Jesus is teaching, which is the seed they are to sow in the world as His followers.

Next He explains the four kinds of soil (people's hearts) on which that seed will fall. First is *the unbroken soil of a hard heart*—soil on a well-traveled path through a field where sown seed lies exposed and cannot germinate. These people hear the word, but they cannot believe and be saved because "the devil comes and takes away the word from their heart" (v. 12). Second is *the uncleared soil of a shallow heart*—soil not cleared of rocks to a depth of six to eight inches, which would allow sufficient root growth. These "receive the word with joy" and "believe for a while" but fall away when tempted because they "have no firm root" (v. 13). Third is *the untilled soil of a divided heart*—soil choked with briars and thorns, leaving no room for anything else to grow. These "bring no fruit to maturity" from the word they hear because their lives are "choked with worries and riches and pleasures of this life" (v. 14).

Fourth, though, is *the cultivated soil of a prepared heart*—"good soil" that is loosened, cleared, and tilled—ready to receive seed. Jesus says, "These are the ones who have heard the word in an honest and good heart, and hold it fast, and bear fruit with perseverance" (v. 15). They are the ones He described earlier who produce "a crop a hundred times as great" (v. 8). This is the kind of soil all lifegiving parents should want for the hearts of their children—that they would hear the truth of God, hold it fast, be spiritually fruitful, and persevere in faith. And this is where it starts to get "good."

Jesus adds something here not mentioned in the other accounts, and it will help answer the question, How does my child's heart become good soil? Jesus says that "good soil" represents a person with "an honest and good heart." He uses two Greek words, both of which can mean "good." *Kalos* often refers to something that is beautiful and praiseworthy—an aesthetic goodness. *Agathos* often refers to something that is useful and beneficial—an ethical goodness. They are common and roughly interchangeable words, but the literal wording of a "good and good" heart suggests the goodness of

God in all its dimensions. That raises another question: Where does that kind of heart come from? Remember, this is a *prepared heart*, but it is also an *unsaved heart*—it has not yet received the word by which it could "believe and be saved" (v. 12).

Jesus suggests that a "good soil" heart is one purposely prepared to receive the seed of the Word because it has been loosened, cleared, and tilled. But He also suggests that in real life, this preparation happens when a heart is taught to value, recognize, and respond to God's goodness in all its expressions. Though it is a sinful, unsaved heart in need of salvation, Jesus says it is nonetheless able to recognize the aesthetic and ethical value of God's goodness, what He describes both as "good soil" and as a "good heart." That kind of heart doesn't happen by accident—it requires intentional preparation. Lifegiving parenting provides the kind of preparation that will help cultivate "an honest and good heart" in your child, a heart attuned to God's goodness and character. And we need to revisit here the wonderful biblical example of heart preparation in the life of Timothy that we touched on in chapter 6.

Timothy lived in Lystra and started following Paul after his second missionary journey there. A number of years later, Paul writes what may have been his final letter from a Roman prison to "Timothy, my beloved son" (2 Timothy 1:2). He reminds Timothy of his upbringing as a child, stating that it was the Word of God sown by the "sincere faith" of his grandmother, Lois, and mother, Eunice (v. 5), that prepared his heart to respond when he heard the gospel. He tells Timothy, "From *childhood* you have known the sacred writings which are able to give you *the wisdom that leads to salvation* through faith which is in Christ Jesus" (3:15, emphasis added). Timothy has known the Old Testament teachings not just as an adult but "from childhood." Paul uses the term *brephos*, which refers to an infant or to a child still in the womb. It's the same word used in Luke to describe John in Elizabeth's womb (1:41) and newborn Jesus in the manger (2:16). The implication is that the soil of Timothy's heart was being prepared for salvation long before he came to faith in Christ. Because of that preparation, the character of his heart was good and the seed of the gospel found good soil, "grew up, and produced a crop a hundred times as great" (8:8).

❧   ❧

Most of what we've covered so far in this book has been, in essence, about cultivating your children's character—nurturing their spirits, guarding their hearts, renewing their minds, strengthening their faith, and training their wills. Or to put it in the language of this chapter, it has been about cultivating the soil of your children's hearts to recognize, value, and know the multifaceted goodness of God (mostly His ethical goodness so far, but chapter 9, on imagination, will touch on His aesthetic goodness). Lifegiving parenting is about influencing your child's "inner person [that] is being renewed day by day" (2 Corinthians 4:16, NET©), which as we've seen in the parable of the Sower and in Timothy's life, can begin in childhood even before your child knows Jesus through personal faith.

Before we move on with this exploration of biblical, or Christian, character for a child, we need to define it. But that's not as easy as it sounds. The term *dokimē*, which is typically translated "character," simply means being tried, tested, or proven—the idea being a person's "proven-ness" (see Romans 5:3-5). But what exactly is being proved that we call character? GotQuestions.org says, "A person's character is the sum of his or her disposition, thoughts, intentions, desires, and actions."[1] A complex interaction of internal values and beliefs influences our choices, which in turn influence our character.

And therein is the rub with defining Christian character, especially for not-yet-proven children—it is not just one thing but the sum of many things in their hearts. However, based on the Sower parable, I believe we can say that valuing God's goodness is the defining element of Christian character, especially for children. So let me take a stab at a definition: Christian character is the moral compass of the heart that guides children's lives and their decisions to pursue excellence and goodness. As we learned in the parable, that character can begin as the "good soil" of a heart prepared to value the goodness of God. When the seed, the gospel of salvation, falls into your children's good heart-soil, Jesus says it will find root and bear fruit "with perseverance." Their moral compasses will find true north in Christ.

Here's what that means for lifegiving parenting. If your children learn godly character qualities from you during childhood, they will simply continue walking in them whenever they accept Jesus as their Savior. The good and godly character you cultivate in them as children will create the "good soil" in their hearts that will at some point become the character of Christ when they become "new creatures" in Him and the Holy Spirit begins working in them (see Galatians 5:22-23; Colossians 3:12-15). Cultivating good character in your children now will keep them on the way of life with God, which will lead them to Jesus, who is "the way, even the truth and the life" (translators' note, John 14:6, NET©). Good soil prepares your children to say yes to Jesus and become more like Him every day. Lifegiving parenting can lead them toward finding new life in Christ, who is the "author of life" (Acts 3:15, NIV).

A caveat about character, though, before we move on. Too many "character building" programs suggest that Christian character is simply the accumulation of many discrete character traits. That assumption can be a form of behaviorism, a materialistic view of human nature that says children come into the world as "blank slates" (*tabulae rasae*) that parents can write on to create whatever kinds of humans they desire. However, that's not true. Children come into this world with a significant amount of programming already on the hard drives of their natures—the presence of God's image; the ability to learn to speak and read; a hunger for knowledge; curiosity and creativity; an openness to parental influence. Cultivating character involves knowing and cooperating with God's preprogrammed design for our children. We don't do this through a method or program, as much as we might want one that will get us off the hook. Instead, we need to be faithful in preparing the soil of our children's hearts, and we trust God with cultivating their character—the moral compass that guides them to value what is good.

Since we've already covered many of the more practical aspects of cultivating good character, such as numbering our children's days, guarding their hearts, and transforming their minds, in this chapter I want to focus instead on some aspects of your child's "inner person" that both grow out of character and form it. I think of these aspects as a kind of internal framework on which good character and the character of Christ are built and supported. I'll mention three—identity (who they are in God's eyes), personality (what they're like by God's design), and capability (what they can do with God's help). Your children are "fearfully and wonderfully made" (Psalm 139:14) by God to be unique blessings to you and others (see Psalm 127:3-5), and their character is inextricably bound up with God's design for them. So the more you can help your children discover and develop what God designed them to be—His children who pursue His goodness—the more confident they will become as followers of Jesus. Let's take a look at those three aspects of your children's internal frameworks and how you can use them to bring God's life into their thinking about God's design for them.

Identity—Telling Your Children Who They Are in God's Eyes

Childhood character is as much about how your children perceive themselves as it is about how they behave and what they believe. It is, at its roots, an inclination of the heart—the internal attitudes, truths, and ideas that motivate and shape your children's choices. In that way, character is spiritually connected to training your children's wills, as discussed in the previous chapter. The will, informed by character, determines choices, which can in turn shape the cores of your children's developing identities. Because of this connection, it is critical you tell your children who they are in God's eyes—that you speak into their lives the words that you want to inform the inclinations of their hearts. By God's design, their hearts—the inner person of their souls—are attuned to you as their parent during childhood, and your words will both form and inform their developing identities to help prepare the soil of their hearts. As a lifegiving parent, you must learn the skill of speaking positive words of life and truth into your children. When it comes to helping your children pursue God's excellence and goodness, there is simply no substitute for the power of your voice telling your children who they are.

It's easy to find Pinterest boards filled with quotes and verses about our identities in Christ as adults. It's not as easy to find material that highlights children's identities in Christ. Much of the content is about what Christ has done for us, but it's expressed in words that are meaningful mostly for mature believers—*justified, forgiven, adopted, redeemed, chosen.* Though children could learn those words, they would struggle to find much meaning in such theologically abstract terms. I'd like to suggest three simpler, more concrete phrases that you can speak into your children's lives that will help shape their identities. Tell them, "You are God's . . . You are loved . . . You are good." Tell them every day. Use those simple anchor words to talk about who they are in God's eyes.

You are God's. "Acknowledge that the LORD is God! *He made us, and we are his.* We are his people, the sheep of his pasture" (Psalm 100:3, NLT; emphasis added). Tell your children they are not only made by God but also belong to Him as their Creator. "You are God's" is the answer to the most fundamental "Who am I?" question we all seek to answer—not just as adults but also as children. Their initial "Where did I come from?" is just a variation on the real "Who am I?" question of their hearts. As you begin to share with them that God made them, you are also sharing what their Maker is like—that He is loving, faithful, kind, generous, safe, powerful, and so much more. Your children will begin to form a foundational understanding of their identities—that they are made by and belong to a God who is good in every way. "You are God's" is a critical piece of their identities and will affect everything that follows.

You are loved. "See *how very much our Father loves us,* for he calls us his children, and that is what we are!" (1 John 3:1, NLT; emphasis added). Tell your children that they are greatly loved by God and by you. "You are loved" reminds them they are lovable, even by themselves. If they know God loves them, then their identities form around an understanding that they are acceptable as they are—they don't need to be something or someone else; they simply need to learn to be who they are, just as God made them. Self-acceptance and emotional security are critical for children growing up in a culture that tells them from an early age that they need to be prettier, stronger, smarter, richer, better—in short, that they need to be something other than they are to be acceptable. "You are loved" is an antidote to those negative messages.

You are good. "I am certain that God, *who began the good work within you,* will continue his work until it is finally finished on the day when Christ Jesus returns" (Philippians 1:6, NLT; emphasis added). Tell your children they are good. Period. This simple, unassuming word is powerful in the hearts of children. "You are good" is a statement not about the absence of sin or of bad behavior but simply about dignity and identity. Though children have sin natures, Scripture teaches childhood innocence, and Jesus affirms that unsaved hearts can value God's goodness. Though Paul is speaking in the verse above to mature believers, "the good work within you" is no less the same heart preparation of childhood that we see in the parable of the Sower. Your children are good because God created them for good, noble, and honorable purposes, He is preparing their hearts with His goodness, and He has begun a "good work" in them. "You are good" is a powerful affirmation that can shape your children's identities with a positive sense of dignity and purpose. How your children understand their natures will shape how they understand the character God is creating within them.

Personality—Telling Your Children What They're Like by God's Design

Scripture contains no discernible doctrine of personality, and yet it permeates every page where we encounter a person in the biblical stories. Scripture may not tell, but certainly shows, the reality of personality. Similarly, there is no medical test that reveals your children's personalities and yet you've been observing them from the day they came out of the womb. The issue is not whether each of your children has a personality, but whether it can be defined in some way, how it might relate to their character, how it helps them understand what they're like by God's design, and how it relates to your responsibilities as a lifegiving parent.

Isabel Briggs Myers, cocreator with her mother of the popular Myers-Briggs Type Indicator (MBTI), said in her book *Gifts Differing*, "Type development starts at a very early age. The hypothesis is that [personality] type is inborn."[2] Myers believed that personality is innate and God given. Her MBTI model of personalities, yielding four general temperaments and sixteen specific types, is consistent with God's creation, which includes variable but limited kinds of animals, birds, insects, and other creatures. It makes sense that we should also be able to discern a limited number of types of personalities in the human realm.

One generally accepted view of personality theory maintains that while children are not mature enough to discern their own personality preferences and traits before their early teens, a parent is able to observe and discern them. The goal is not to put boxes around your children but rather to help them understand and be comfortable with their own God-given personalities and to appreciate personalities different than their own. A second goal is to help you, as a parent, differentiate between your children's personality traits and character traits. One helpful way to make that distinction is to imagine that personality is the clothing that character wears in public. For example, extroverted children might express care for a friend differently than introverted children, but they are both expressing the character trait of loving others.

Christian parents can use a variety of personality models, some specifically designed for children and others designed for adults but then applied to children. Any can be helpful if used appropriately and if the language and model are accessible for children. Sally and I were influenced by the MBTI, enough that I became qualified to administer it, but we also used a personality-type model that applied children-friendly language to learning styles, which I developed specifically for our ministry. My model identified four "wholehearted" temperaments:

The **DOER child**—the industrious child who gets things done. "I can do that!"

The **HELPER child**—the serving child who encourages others. "How can I help you?"

The **MOVER child**—the inspiring child who influences others. "Let's do it together."

The **SHAPER child**—the imaginative child who conceives new things. "I have a better idea."

I included additional factors for "Mental Focus" (active or reflective) and "Life Orientation" (time or experience) to help sharpen the personality assessment, but the four primary types are the starting point. (See "Knowing Your Child's Personality" on pages 221–26 for more on personality.)

There's one other factor you should consider in understanding your child's personality—your own personality! A dynamic that happens between different personality types can be good or bad—some types get along well, others not so well. You'll see that dynamic interplay among your children, but you should also be aware of it between you and each of your children. For instance, if you are very outgoing (an Active Doer) and your child is quiet and reserved (a Reflective Mover), your personality might mistake your child's for being reclusive or lazy. Such an assessment moves beyond personality into character, which isn't fair or appropriate. Or if you are very orderly and punctual (a Time-Oriented Shaper) and your child is relational and spontaneous (an Experience-Oriented Helper), you might be tempted to assess their character as flighty and irresponsible. You need to learn to distinguish between personality traits and character traits.

One side reason, then, for studying personality is to neutralize those kinds of personality issues that might otherwise result in misdirected character assessments, whether by your children or by you. However, the primary reason to study personality is to help your children know what they're like by God's design. Personality is part of your child's "inner person" that you need to understand in order to effectively cultivate character. You cannot simply dismiss or ignore your children's personalities—they need to be a part of how you relate to them as a lifegiving parent. Since God personally designed your children and "made all the delicate, inner parts of [their] body and knit [them] together in [their] mother's womb" (Psalm 139:13, NLT), then when you affirm their personalities, you are recognizing the fingerprints of God on their very inner beings, the life marks of the One who made them the way they are. It is their God-given personalities that will bring life to the character that God is developing within them. What could be more lifegiving than that?

Capability—Telling Your Children What They Can Do with God's Help

Children should not have to be burdened with poor self-esteem or a low estimation of their own self-worth because of negative impacts from home life, economic constraints, educational challenges, physical issues, and more. Public school self-esteem programs attempt to fill in the cracks of children's distorted self-perceptions created by a broken and lonely modern culture. However, catchy slogans, colorful workbooks, and positive self-talk can only go so far to remedy those real and often intractable problems and to overcome spiritual and psychic wounds.

As a lifegiving Christian parent, you have the opportunity to protect your children from the negative effects of modern culture that wound so many other children's spirits. That alone is a beautiful gift you can give to your children, and through them to the world. However, you will still need to work to ensure they have an internal sense of personal security and a positive self-worth—it won't happen automatically just because they grow up in a Christian home, or even because you help them know their identities in Christ. Cultivating character requires more than just internal affirmations of goodness and worth.

A full sense of self-worth includes your children knowing they have God-given capabilities, ones He can use for His purposes and glory—capabilities to make the world better, to help another person, to create something valuable, or to encourage others. You can build foundations for your children's character by strengthening their identities and understanding their personalities, but those are more internal qualities. Capability looks outward. If identity is about loving *God* and personality is about loving *self*, then capability is about loving *others* (see Matthew 22:34-40). It's about channeling character to serve, help, love, encourage, and give.

Charlotte Mason (1842–1923) was a turn-of-the-century British educator and author who greatly influenced the overinstitutionalized and soulless education system of her day. One of her innovations was to view the child as a real person capable of self-directed learning. Her motto for her students was "I am. I can. I ought. I will." It expressed much the same idea as the concept of capability. She saw in children an unlimited capacity to learn that needed to be nurtured and stimulated, not controlled and conformed. She wanted to retrain the self-perception and self-worth of the beleaguered student masses of her day by affirming and releasing their own native capabilities to learn and do by their own motivation and character. She recognized the power of self-perception and capability to shape the character of a child.

Your children have natural, God-given talents, skills, and abilities that are waiting to be affirmed and released—perhaps in music, art, math, design, computer programming, helping, leading, cooking, and many more areas. Your great privilege and responsibility is to recognize special capabilities in your children and then encourage those abilities, provide ways to develop them, and engage them in ways that will serve and help others. When you tell your children what they can do with God's help, you are acknowledging God has given them special capabilities that they can choose to use for Him. You are cultivating their character by helping them see their capabilities as a gift from God—a stewardship that He has entrusted to them to faithfully manage, develop, and use for His glory. It may be that you are developing in them what later will become a spiritual gift to edify the body of Christ. The sense of self-worth that comes from knowing that God has personally designed you with skills and capabilities He can use for His glory needs no slogans and posters—it needs only affirmation, direction, and release.

Perhaps more than self-esteem, what many wounded children need is a sense of self-confidence—knowing they have something worthy of developing and using in service of others. When children have self-confidence, they are better equipped to avoid the speed bumps, potholes, and pitfalls of life. Even though your children may find the roads of life relatively smooth, they will be no less influenced by the power of self-confidence. The more they develop their God-given capabilities, the more they will increase their capacities to act. That growth in capability will increase their self-confidence and give them a stronger sense of their self-worth.

Identity, personality, and capability all create frameworks within which you can cultivate your children's character and help them learn to pursue what is good and excellent. When you tell your children what they can do with God's help, you are connecting them with the living God who will help. That is lifegiving parenting.

⸙

We've covered a lot of ground in this chapter talking about what it means to cultivate character in your child. At its most basic level, cultivating character is influencing your child's heart, or inner person, to value and desire the goodness of God—everything about Him that is aesthetically good (all that is beautiful and praiseworthy) and ethically good (all that is beneficial and true). Metaphorically, it means your children, with your lifegiving assistance, are setting the moral compass of their hearts by God's goodness, the spiritual equivalent of true north. All the lifegiving heartbeats we looked at before this chapter explained various ways you can contribute to your children's developing character.

Despite all that input, though, character is still a mysterious quality in your child. But Jesus has a good word for you as one of His disciples. Even though understanding of His parables was not given to those who did not choose to follow Him, Jesus says, "To you it has been granted to know the mysteries of the kingdom of God" (Luke 8:10). As a follower of Christ, you are among those who can see and understand the radical messages of Jesus' parables, such as His teaching in the parable of the Sower about the "good soil" of an "honest and good heart" (v. 15).

If the Sower parable includes children's hearts, as I believe it does, then Jesus' instruction for you as a lifegiving parent is clear: Your responsibility is to keep the soil of your children's hearts loosened, tilled, cleared, cultivated, and fed with the goodness of God so they will also be among those "who have heard the word in an honest and good heart, and hold it fast, and bear fruit with perseverance" (v. 15). Those are words all lifegiving parents should want said of their children. When you cultivate your children's character with the goodness of God, you are introducing them to the fullest expression of life that God has to offer to all of us. The Kingdom of God has come to your home.

Sally's Lifegiving Momoirs

When Joel was about eleven years old, I thought he would enjoy being involved in a local boys' choir in Fort Worth, Texas, where we were living at that time. He had been musical from a very young age, singing on pitch from around eighteen months and making music throughout childhood. I thought being in the boys' choir would give him an opportunity to receive some formal musical training and immerse himself in a structured musical experience. When he auditioned, the choir director said he could not trip up Joel on any of the melodic and harmonic tests, and he was very positive about Joel being part of the choir.

As Joel got involved and received attention from the director, an older and much bigger boy of thirteen, who was about to graduate from the group, began to bully Joel. He was mean to him, pushing him around during breaks and telling him he wasn't really that good. Joel reported to us what was happening, and we said we'd talk to the choir director about it. Joel went to a couple more rehearsals before the appointment, and one night when Clay was out of town, he came to my bedroom and wanted to talk about the boy. Joel said he'd found out from another friend in the choir that the older boy's father had recently left his family and that they had been forced to move out of their house and into a small apartment. He told me, "Mama, that would make me so sad and angry. Maybe that's why the boy is being mean to me. I think I just need to be patient and kind to him, because that's what Jesus would want me to do."

This was a moment when Joel decided to choose to have character like Jesus so he could be a witness and help to this boy. Clay and I were ready to go to the director, but Joel wanted to handle the situation privately. It was a testimony of his developing Christian character and showed he'd been listening to our family devotions and discussions about humility and serving others.

Joel eventually went on to study composition at Berklee College of Music and developed a special interest in choral composition. The music world is filled with difficult personalities and strong egos, so that early training in choosing character over confrontation prepared him well for a career in music.

Lifegiving ParenTips

The beauty of God's goodness. We talked earlier in the chapter about character growing out of our valuing and desiring God's goodness expressed in truth and beauty. Many Christian parents are comfortable telling their children about the beneficial goodness of God's truth—how it is a source of blessing, pleases God, directs us, corrects us, protects us, and more. Concrete and propositional truths are easy. However, most parents probably are not as comfortable telling their children about the praiseworthy goodness of God's beauty. Abstract and intangible concepts are more of a challenge. And yet Jesus seems to indicate that the "good soil" of an "honest and good heart" is cultivated by valuing both truth and beauty. So make time to value the goodness of God's beauty in your home. Listen to beautiful and uplifting music of all kinds (classical, solo instrumental, vocal, acoustic); look at books of beautiful artwork and photographs of nature with your children; read inspiring and beautifully written literature aloud; set aside nights to read inspiring poetry by the best poets; read psalms aloud and listen for the beauty of the Hebraic thoughts and language. Beauty is good, and it builds character.

The joy of personality. Our family, even when the kids were young, loved to talk about and compare personalities. There was something about sharing the "who, what, and why are you" of personality that we all found enjoyable and affirming as a family. No personality type was considered better or worse than any other, and no critical comments were allowed. There was a definite sense of "pride of ownership" for our children as they were able to name, describe, and good-heartedly defend their personality types and preferences to siblings and parents, complete with humorous admissions of their own personality quirks and weaknesses. Our family mostly used MBTI with its four-letter labels that, once mastered, are incredibly informative, but any personality model that everyone can understand and enjoy will do. Some children might especially enjoy personality profiles based on animal types (dogs, cats, mammals, insects) or on characters from children's stories (Winnie the Pooh, Narnia, Beatrice Potter). So set aside a night, put out some hot chocolate and a good treat, and celebrate the different ways that God has created you and your children.

The ability to be capable. Part of the internal framework on which to cultivate good character in your children is helping them discover the special capabilities God has given them—the skills, abilities, and talents that make them unique and special. More important than having those capabilities, though, is learning how to give them away—to use them for God's glory to serve, help, and encourage others. That's where you come in as a lifegiving parent. First, do whatever you can to help your children develop their capabilities—perhaps through quality lessons, a class or workshop, tools and resources you can acquire, or a project they can work on. Next, encourage them to think of ways that God might use their skills or talents to minister to others. Resist the urge to offer your own ideas; let your children come up with them. Finally, look for ways to make those ideas happen when they're ready. They might perform music at a nursing home, build birdhouses for neighbors, knit scarves for friends, create newsletters for Sunday school, play instruments for children's worship, create plays for friends, read aloud to homeless children, or make muffins for shut-ins. It will all help cultivate character in their hearts.

Starting the Heartbeat of Parental Lifegiving

Cultivating your child's character starts with preparing the soil of your child's heart to receive God's truth. Christian character comes from giving your child a heart that values the goodness of God, expressed in good and godly identity, personality, and capability.

CHAPTER 9

FORMING YOUR CHILD'S IMAGINATION

You will keep in perfect peace all who trust in you,
all whose thoughts are fixed on you!

ISAIAH 26:3, NLT

IMAGINATION IS THE BRIGHTLY colored thread running through the textured tapestry of our family stories. On the front of the tapestry, the thread flows in well-behaved waves of color through each child's story line, bursting into woven images of art, people, faith, words, music, life, and more. But turn the tapestry over, and the view is different. There, all those seemingly civilized threads of imagining become a riotous explosion of tangled colors. There's more behind every tapestry image than what you can see only on the surface. That's been the story of our family.

Sally and I never sat down together to create a plan to make our children imaginative and creative. We did, though, deliberately create an atmosphere that was rich in spoken and printed words—reading books, discussing everything, engaging with art and beauty. Creativity was the air our children breathed in our home, and imagination is what came out when they exhaled. They didn't have to study imagination; they simply grew up in soil that fed it and allowed it to bloom.

When Sarah was about nine, she wrote a lengthy story about her My Little Pony—an enthralling tale about herself and a magical, talking, flying unicorn saving their friends through a magic portal in a hidden cave. She wrote her story with no prompting or help, revealing it only after it was completed, when she asked if she could read it to us. It was just a childhood exercise in storytelling at the time, and yet Sarah remembers it as her first taste of writing that lit a fire that still burns brightly.

Joel was always reading, thinking, and drawing. When we found a small motorized riding jeep, he was captivated. The yard-sale jeep soon died, but not his vision and imagination for what a jeep should be. He quite literally spent hours drawing hundreds of jeeps in all shapes, styles, and sizes, with innovations and special features. He read books on cars and jeeps to feed his imagination so he could make his jeeps better. That same attention to detail and innovation later segued into his being able to compose and orchestrate complicated pieces of music.

Nathan loved dressing up as heroes, literary characters, and historical figures. When he was about ten, he and his best friend from next door played in a treehouse they'd built on the hill behind our houses. One day Nathan asked if he could read us a poem he had written. "What Will the Treehouse Be Today?" was an imaginative series of ponderings: Will it be a pirate ship? Will it be a castle? Will it be a rocket ship? The poem was several pages long, illustrated with detailed drawings. I can't help but think it was early practice for storyboarding, a skill he would need for making movies as a young adult.

Then there was Joy, also a prime pretender. We moved to Nashville when Joy was seven years old. She had her own room that was only as big as an oversized closet, but it was her private world. Sally read

Little House on the Prairie to her, and something in it sparked Joy's imagination. She began to create her own hand-drawn, multipage weekly "newspapers," each with a masthead, columns, news stories, advertisements, and drawings. She created a weekly writing schedule just like a real reporter. Her weekly "Joynal" was certainly early training in creativity, diligence, and careful use of words—qualities that helped her later when she competed in speech and debate.

Those are some quick glimpses of how imagination played out in the Clarkson home. Like colored thread in a tapestry, it ran through everything and everyone. However, our story is just one of many testimonies of the life-shaping power of imagination for children in countless other families like ours. I share our stories not to suggest that our family experience is any kind of ideal model to emulate but rather simply to illustrate the importance of forming your children's imaginations. Don't neglect it, even if it seems unimportant to you. Imagine that it isn't.

It's appropriate that the final lifegiving heartbeat chapter in this book is about forming your children's imaginations. First, because it is only by imagination that we as parents will be able to envision the kind of lives we can give to our children. We're motivated by our hopes about what kinds of people they'll become—how they'll use their gifts and talents, what kinds of spouses and parents they'll be, how they'll make their marks for God's Kingdom. Second, it's only by a Christ-formed imagination that our children will be able to see what we envision for them. Their imaginations need to be formed and fed to realize the vision for what they can become in God's grand story. In other words, imagination is a symbiotic process in family— we imagine so they can imagine.

That's why I'm asking you to use your imagination as you read, allowing you to see more than just the limited words on these few pages. I also hope you'll consider this chapter as a mental and spiritual primer for your own study and thinking about imagination. The rest of this chapter will answer four questions: What is imagination? What does Scripture say about imagination? Why is imagination important for my child? How is imagination formed in my child?

What Is Imagination?

Imagination is one of those words we use somewhat carelessly. We know what we mean by it, but only in a casual, colloquial sense. Books have been written on the physiological, philosophical, sociological, and theological dimensions of the mental faculty of imagination, but few of us will have the time or inclination to explore those aspects of our children's minds in detail. Many in the church, from the early church fathers forward, cautioned against engaging the imagination, which they viewed with suspicion—sometimes even considering it a dangerous alliance with spirits and ungodly images. Until the mid-1800s, children were discouraged from reading "imaginative" stories such as fantasies and fairy tales. However, a renewed interest in the *imago Dei* (Latin for "image of God") we all possess has restored our trust in imagination and introduced the language of a redeemed, or Christian, imagination.

According to Merriam-Webster.com, imagination is "the act or power of forming a mental image of something not present to the senses or never before wholly perceived in reality."[1] It involves seeing things in the mind that may or may not exist in the material world. When you read your children a story about a dragon, their minds imagine a dragon of some kind; they naturally convert language into a mental image. C. S. Lewis got that picture: "For me, reason is the natural organ of truth; but *imagination is the organ of meaning*. Imagination . . . is not the cause of truth, but its condition."[2] To say it another way, your children will understand abstract words and concepts by reason but will also assign meaning to them in their imaginations through images, metaphors, symbols, and story.

Imagination is remarkably uncomplicated for children—it is

a natural, transparent ability. They don't have to understand it or be taught how to imagine; they just do it. But in order to become healthy and strong parts of their human nature, their imaginations must be fed and formed. And if they are to become well-formed "Christian imaginations," they must be tended purposely to that end. That's our responsibility as lifegiving parents. Our children's natural, innocent curiosities are not just seeking reasonable explanations for all their questions; they are also seeking meaning. A Christian imagination enables our children not only to see God's truth through images, metaphors, and symbols but also to see themselves as part of a grand story being written by God, a story that brings ultimate meaning to everything.

In the same way that Jesus is the incarnated Word of God (John 1:14), we are in some mysterious way an incarnation of God's divine *imagination* (2 Corinthians 5:17), connected to Him by His *image* within us (Genesis 1:27). God never tells us exactly what that image is, but the view that makes sense to me sees it as our nature as created human beings who exist in meaningful relationship with God and others—the quality that makes us distinct from the rest of creation. Think of the *imago Dei* as a magnet in our natures that draws us into relationships. When we form our children's Christian imaginations, we're drawing them to the life of God in us, in others, and in themselves.

What Does Scripture Say about Imagination?

We can't understand the Word of God without a well-formed imagination. From Genesis to Revelation, the Bible is filled with prophetic images, theological metaphors, truth-revealing symbols, and allegorical stories. The images of Genesis 1–3 invite us to visualize the creation of the world, the first man and woman, and the corruption of Paradise by a talking serpent. The images and symbols of Revelation challenge us to imagine the end of history, the defeat of evil, and the beginning of a new heaven and a new earth. In between, we're pulled into a story of sin, sacrifice, and redemption as big as time and creation, but as personal as a man dying on a cross out of love for the world. It's about a King and a Kingdom; spiritual battles in the air, on the earth, and in the heart; and the Holy Breath giving us divine power to serve our King. The story is imagined by a transcendent God who is our Father, an eternal Savior who is His Son, a body of people who are a bride, and a spiritual house full of adopted children.

Scripture assumes and generously affirms the faculty of the imagination throughout both testaments. And yet only a few words in Hebrew and Greek are directly translatable into English as "imagine" or "imagination." Nonetheless, the lack of specific terms does not minimize the presence of imaginative language and concepts on nearly every page of the Bible. One interesting Hebrew term to consider is *yatsar*, which can mean "to form or fashion in the mind"—to frame, conceive, or imagine something unseen as real and true.

Consider Isaiah's familiar words: "The steadfast of mind You will keep in perfect peace, because he trusts in You" (Isaiah 26:3). The word translated as "mind" is the noun form of the verb *yatsar*—meaning this phrase could be translated "the steadfast of *imagination*." Isaiah says God's peace, His *shalom*, will come to those whose imaginations are supported and firm. In the larger context (25:6–26:6), Isaiah charges the people of Judah to imagine "that day" when God will "swallow up death for all time . . . wipe tears away from all faces, and . . . remove the reproach of His people from all the earth" (25:8). He asks them to *yatsar* a future reality, to look beyond their rational intellects in order to frame the future by what they see with their imaginations. If "faith is being sure of what we hope for and certain of what we do not see" (Hebrews 11:1, NIV), then strongly supported imaginations will enable your children to see, by faith, what God has yet to bring about.

The New Testament is abundantly rich in the language of faith and belief, which assume imagination. The words of Jesus serve as the best example. His Sermon on the Mount (Matthew 5–7) begins with concepts that are as abstract as they are concrete, that ask us to imagine the kinds of people He has come to bless and the kind of world He promises to them: "Blessed are the poor in spirit, for theirs is the kingdom of heaven. . . . Blessed are the gentle, for they shall inherit the earth. . . . Blessed are the pure in heart, for they shall see God" (5:3, 5, 8). His parables engage the imagination like few stories ever written: the Prodigal Son, the Sower, the Good Samaritan, the Ten Talents, the Laborers in the Vineyard, and so many others. He uses metaphors to picture truth about His nature and mission, calling Himself the Good Shepherd, the Light of the World, the Bread of Life, the Living Water. He also uses riddles and images—such as the Kingdom of Heaven, sheep and goats, a mustard seed, being born again, the eye of a needle, "the last shall be first," vines and branches. His miracles and healings are images and symbols of truth—turning water into wine, multiplying loaves and fishes, raising Lazarus, healing the paralyzed man lowered on a pallet, calming the storm, exorcising demons, and many more.

We haven't even scratched the surface, but I hope this brief overview of imagination in Scripture will challenge your *yatsar* to frame in your mind a picture of how imagination relates to you as a life-giving parent. The New Testament is rich in the language of belief and the motif of imagination. If you want your children to engage the Bible with understanding of all it has to offer, you need to think about what it means to form their imaginations. It won't happen unless you imagine it first.

Why Is Imagination Important for My Child?

Each of our children experienced doubt at some point during their youth. We didn't consider it a failure of our spiritual parenting but rather a natural part of their maturation and faith experience. It meant they were thinking deeply about what they believed, wanting to own their beliefs. We would pray with them, share Scripture, and talk through their concerns, but sometimes that wasn't enough. One of our children, though very knowledgeable about Scripture, went through an extended period of private doubt in the late teens, struggling to make sense of Christianity and life. Later we would learn what "saved" this child from doubts—imagination. Specifically, it was reading J. R. R. Tolkien's fantasy trilogy, The Lord of the Rings. This child found in Tolkien's epic story of goodness overcoming evil a literary parallel to the divine metanarrative of the Bible, an imaginative path to finding a place in God's epic story of creation, fall, redemption, and restoration. The story of Frodo, Sam, Gandalf, Aragorn, and all the others involved in the struggle for Middle Earth proved to be a lifegiving metaphor of this child's own struggle to find a place in God's story. Imagination is important.

Most Christian parents do not fear imagination, but neither do they especially respect its power in children's lives. It's easy to wrongly assign it to the category of pleasant childhood diversions that will pass in time as their children grow into young adulthood. But children's developing imaginations need to be properly fed in order to grow into mature imaginations that can anchor the deepest, most meaningful concepts in Scripture. A faith that is uninformed or uninspired by the images, metaphors, symbols, and stories of God's Word is in danger of becoming unimaginative and unanchored, weakened by an overreliance on reason, adrift on a shallow sea of facts and propositions. God *imagined* the entirety of creation in eternity past before He ever spoke the first "Let there be . . ." of His epic story, creating every micro and macro part of His infinitely complex, undeniably beautiful and "good" creation. He left His signature on His work in the *imago Dei* that's written indelibly on our souls. We dare not fail to respect the power of His imagination in us or our children.

Imagination is important for our children for one overriding reason—it is the faculty by which they will believe. It's easy to make the mistake of thinking that imagination, like inspiration, is a kind of passive mental state. Rather, it is more like a muscle that will become stronger or weaker depending on how it is fed, exercised, and used. Christian author Caryn Rivadeneira makes the faith connection: "Without imagination—without the ability to picture what is unseen, to believe what is unknown—how can we have faith? Without imagination, without the ability to imagine a 'preferred future,' how can we hope? Without imagination, how can we experience the majesty and wonder and nearness of a mysterious God?"[3]

The world says, "You've got to see it to believe it," but biblical belief turns that on its head, saying, "You've got to believe it to see it." In other words, there is a kind of seeing that starts with belief: "Now faith is the assurance of things hoped for, the *conviction of things not seen*" (Hebrews 11:1, emphasis added). The author of Hebrews asserts that the "conviction" of faith, or belief, enables us to see the "not seen" things of God. Similarly, Paul prays that God will give the Ephesians spiritual eyes—eyes of the heart—to see all that He has done for us as believers: "I pray that the *eyes of your heart* may be enlightened, so that you will know what is the hope of His calling, what are the riches of the glory of His inheritance in the saints, and what is the surpassing greatness of His power toward us who believe" (Ephesians 1:18-19, emphasis added; see also 1 Corinthians 2:6-13). If you want your children to "see" all the unseen ways God tells us He blesses His children now and in eternity, a well-formed Christian imagination is the starting place.

Henry David Thoreau, a nineteenth-century author, naturalist, and poet, said, "It's not what you look at that matters, it's what you see." Two people can look at the same pretty flower and "see" different things—one a pleasant happenstance of nature, the other a beautiful piece of artwork by the Creator. The difference is imagination. When you form your children's imaginations, you are training them to see more than just what is there—to look at the world, nature, people, and even daily life with the same eyes of the heart that God gives us to see His redemptive work in eternity. The apostle Paul exhorted, "Set your mind on the things above, not on the things that are on earth" (Colossians 3:2). He commands us to be "minded" about the things above that we can see only with eyes of the heart, not the things below that we see with the eyes in our heads. To obey Paul's command for your children means giving them more than a rational faith—it means also giving them a well-formed Christian imagination that can look at a starry night sky and see more than the infinite reach of empty space and the eternal stretch of endless time, that can "keep seeking the things above, where Christ is, seated at the right hand of God" (v. 1). You are giving your children eyes to see and believe.

How Is Imagination Formed in My Child?

Imagination is not a skill that can be taught, tested, and mastered like concepts from math, language arts, or even drawing. It is not linear but develops organically and globally, like a plant that must be continually fed and tended. Developing a child's imagination is like cultivating the good heart-soil that we talked about in chapter 8. Imagination is a quality of your child's inner life, and as such it should be considered a living thing.

British educator Charlotte Mason viewed imagination as a kind of unlimited renewable resource: "Imagination has the property of magical expansion, the more it holds the more it will hold."[4] Though there are no last-century studies to prove her educational maxim, modern metrics suggest that certain limitations may affect imagination. Results from the Torrance Tests of Creative Thinking (TTCT) have been compiled since 1960, tracking the creativity of millions of elementary (K–6) children. Up until 1990, creativity had increased annually for thirty years; since 1990, it has been steadily declining annually.[5] Reasons for the decrease are unknown, but the advent of computers, video games, tablets, and devices—and the rapid acceptance of their use with children—is the suspected culprit. Perhaps we should add a chilling corollary to Mason's maxim: "The more imagination holds, the more it will hold—except to the degree that it is distracted and weakened by passive consumption of too much meaningless activity and content that degrades imagination by mental starvation."

If that corollary is true, as I believe it is, then every lifegiving parent is on notice—only we can form and feed our children's imaginations to be healthy and strong for God. We talked in chapter 2 about numbering our children's days during the brief window of opportunity called childhood. With this final heartbeat chapter, we come full circle. We get no redos if we neglect to form our children's imaginations during the short season of their childhood. As we close this chapter, I want to suggest three general priorities you can begin to implement to help ensure you send your children into young adulthood with well-formed imaginations that are able to enter into the wonder and mystery of God's story.

Make Room for Imagination

The information age has created a frog-in-the-kettle experience for all of us, but especially for children. Like the frog unable to realize the increasing temperature of the water it sits in until it's too late, we're unable to register the increasing information overload as our brains overheat. Recent research indicates that in the 1970s the average person was exposed to only about fifty advertising messages per day, but that had risen to about five thousand by 2006. Other studies suggest an exponential increase in all kinds of daily sensory impressions over the past century, and with the advent of the information age, the Internet, smartphones, and ubiquitous digital devices, there seems to be no end in sight. Children's brains can become so overcrowded with meaningless information that good thoughts can have a hard time breaking free from the increasingly cluttered cognitive space.

What does that information overload mean for you as you work to form your children's imaginations? Let's start with the positive side of the information equation—majoring on the good stuff and minoring on the fun stuff. The "good stuff" involves feeding their brains with the very best food you can—a good version of the Bible, the best Bible storybooks, the best in traditional children's illustrated storybooks, classical children's literature, Christian allegory or fantasy (such as The Chronicles of Narnia), church history and Christian biographies, historical hero stories, beautiful art and photography books, and the best in all genres of music (for additional suggestions, see *Read for the Heart* by Sarah Clarkson). Give your children easy access to all the good stuff in your home. Let them feed on it at will whenever they have free time to choose to fill their minds with it. The "fun stuff" to minor on can be imaginative media that is harmless but not necessarily helpful for feeding the imagination, whether print, music, video, or online. The key word is "minor"— consider it a treat, decide what you'll enjoy and when, and restrict your entertainment intake. The limits are especially important for your children. Don't let the fun stuff push the good stuff aside out of convenience or neglect.

Then there's the negative side of the information equation— constraining the shiny stuff and restraining the empty stuff. The "shiny stuff" is any kind of screen—television, monitor, laptop, tablet, phablet, smartphone, other handheld devices, and more. Some of those devices can be good and can offer meaningful content and healthy interaction, but you should offer them to your children with great restraint and only for use under your supervision. It goes against the cultural tide, but in my opinion, children and younger teens do not need their own cell phones or tablets, as this generally leads to much higher rates of technology consumption. Then there's the "empty stuff" that must be restrained—the commercial, substandard, derivative, meaningless, empty twaddle that some children consume like sugared cereal, whether it is "Christian" or just worldly. Note that using screens even for a supposedly good digital experience trains your children's brains to want more of the experience, with or without the good content. Research is showing that screen engagement has a detrimental effect on children's brain functioning and can act like an addictive drug. Some screens will grab your children's total attention, turn off their imaginations, and fill them with empty clutter and clatter. Avoid those at all costs.

Make Conversation about Imagination

A recent and statistically large study of 8,650 two-year-olds, conducted by researchers at Pennsylvania State University; the University of California, Irvine; and Columbia University, concluded that "children entering kindergarten with higher reading and math achievements are more likely to go to college, own homes, be married, and live in higher-income neighbourhoods as adults."[6] Several studies on adults also show a relationship between a larger vocabulary and intelligence, competence, and success. However, simple common sense also reaches the same conclusion: Good vocabulary makes you smarter. And apart from the intelligence factor associated with vocabulary, the important insight for this book cannot be understated—a larger vocabulary is critical to an active and healthy imagination.

Children's abilities to imagine things beyond what their senses tell them are directly related to the depth and breadth of their vocabularies. It takes very little imagination to realize the negative effects of a limited vocabulary on imagination or belief in spiritual truths and concepts. The more words your children have with which to form and express thoughts, questions, opinions, and insights, the greater will be the scope and intensity of what they can imagine. The stronger your children's grasp of language, the richer will be their own imaginations and ability to wonder about things beyond their five senses. Words mean things—words give content to imagination, and imagination brings meaning to words.

How can you help build your children's vocabularies? The most effective way is not through *Sesame Street*, flash cards, colorful workbooks, or children's apps. Words separated from their uses and meanings in real life are just text without context. Vocabulary is built best by creating a verbal and literary culture in your home. In our family we discussed topics all the time and in every place (see Deuteronomy 6:4-9), and we tried to avoid talking down to our children with simplified vocabulary unless it was to help them understand a difficult word or concept. We offered stories, metaphors, symbols, and illustrations. We did our best to talk about the story of Scripture from all its angles—historical, poetic, narrative, theological, metaphorical, personal. We talked about child-relevant news, the events of our days, random ideas, and opinions. Our children retained new words naturally, hearing them in the real-life contexts that made them meaningful. We also tried to enrich our children's lives with a steady diet of literature, regularly reading books aloud as a family and talking about them, or listening to audiobooks. Quality reading materials were available everywhere in our home. A good vocabulary will grow in the enriched soil of a verbal home.

Make Use of Imagination

The third priority of forming your children's imaginations is the most obvious—put them to use! Some suggest that nearly all children start kindergarten full of natural creativity, but by second or third grade many lose the creative impulse. Why would this happen? Most agree that children's need to conform to the expectations of teachers and classrooms trains them to be compliant, not creative. Freedom surrenders to conformity. Your home should be known not for your children conforming to strict rules and parental expectations but for its love, freedom, creativity, and childlike faith. That does not mean your home should be free of biblical childhood discipline! Quite the opposite, in fact. It is discipline, understood correctly, that provides the structure children need and want and within which grace, truth, love, and freedom can flourish—a secure and safe place where your children's imaginations can be formed, fed, and freed to explore life to the fullest.

Sally and I determined early on in our parenting journey to see our home as more than just a place to live, eat, and sleep. We believed we were cooperating with God's design for the home to be the primary place of influence where our children would find all they needed to become mature, confident, competent, faithful adults. We also tried to give them enjoyable, self-directed, and personally rewarding ways to make use of their imaginations. We created numerous "discovery corners" in our home, each supplied with the books, tools, and resources our children needed to explore the topic of that corner, such as drawing and design, creative play, music making, nature, astronomy, and more. Over the years we also built our family library, decorated our walls with interesting art and Scripture calligraphy, enjoyed a wide variety of music, made holidays times of redemptive creativity (see Sally and Sarah's book, *The Lifegiving Home*), and tried to make every meal a time of both creative and spiritual refreshment (see Sally's book *The Lifegiving Table*).

Forming and feeding our children's imaginations is wonderful, but our challenge is also to expand them. Some children seem to start with a larger natural *capacity* for imagination than others, but every child shares the same *capability* for it—it is part of the image of God in them. But keep in mind that in our digital age, children can passively engage in what seem like imaginative activities yet never really exercise their imaginative muscles. Analog imaginative exercises, in contrast, will be arguably more effective than digital ones. There will be plenty of time for digital engagement when your children are older. We get only one shot at their childhoods, so we must make the most of it by using the natural means God has built into our human experience to grow and expand our children's imaginations. Here are some "back to basics" ideas to get you started.

- *Writing.* When your children are writing freely, give each one a cool journal and a nice pen. Encourage them to write something original or creative in their journals every day. It can be a little or a lot; fiction, fact, fancy, or fantasy; but it must be their own.
- *Drawing.* Give each of your children a sketchbook and a set of good drawing pencils and colored pencils. Every day, have them sketch something they envision in their minds, read in a story, or see in nature, whether real or made up.
- *Telling.* Set aside a few minutes each day for your children to tell you stories, to put into their own words what is in their minds. It can be an original story, a retelling of history, narrating part of a book they're reading, or the kernel of a story idea they're still pondering.
- *Showing.* Periodically set aside time to allow your children to demonstrate and explain something they are working on, thinking about, or engaged in doing. Encourage them to use props and drawings to illustrate what they want to communicate.

If your children need some help getting started, you might create a box with slips of paper on which you write creative suggestions such as "Describe your favorite day," "Write about a trip to Mars," "Draw yourself as an adult," or "Draw a frankentail bird." Your creativity seeds will also show your children your own imagination.

❧ ❧

Forming your children's imaginations is a distinctly lifegiving part of your parenting that connects your children with the life of God. You are putting them in touch with the image of God within them, which connects them with the living God who put it there. This lifegiving heartbeat is unique in that respect, but there is more to it.

The real impact of forming and feeding your children's imaginations is less about what imagination is and how it works and much more about what it enables and where it leads and how that can change your children's lives. I'm convinced that a well-formed imagination is a bridge to an expanded understanding of life that can shape and influence everything your grown children will do—their choices, attitudes, vocations, service, marriages, parenting. On the other side of that bridge are three words that can make that kind of difference— *faith*, *story*, and *Kingdom*.

Faith is belief in what Scripture teaches about God, Jesus, the Holy Spirit, the plan of salvation, spiritual warfare, heaven, and all the abstract truths the Bible tells us are as real as the people of God with whom we believe. Imagination is the corrective lens that enables the believer to "see" those things that are only visible with the eyes of the heart. When we form our children's imaginations, we help them bring into focus with their heart-eyes all the truths and mysteries of the living God that will shape the rest of their lives.

Story is the spiritual emulsifier that brings together all the incredible parts and pieces of our faith into one epic narrative in which we each play a role. As our daughter Sarah wrote in her final paper for graduation from Oxford, "To believe in Christ is to be given a new identity as a protagonist within the ongoing story of redemption, in which our love, action, and hope play a part in the kingdom come." When you form your children's imaginations, you are helping them see themselves as part of a grand story that God has written and is writing—one that will define who they are, not just in this world but in eternity.

Kingdom, then, is the ultimate end of faith and story. In Matthew's Gospel, the first recorded words of Jesus after He returns from the wilderness to begin His earthly ministry are "Repent, for the kingdom of heaven is at hand" (Matthew 4:17). More than fifty times in Matthew, Jesus mentions the gospel of "the kingdom of heaven" or some variation. "Your kingdom come" (6:10) is part of the Lord's Prayer recited weekly by millions of Christians. "Kingdom" is a recurring theme in every Gospel, the book of Acts, the writings of Paul, and the Revelation of John. Why is this Kingdom good news? Because it marks the restoration of the promise of God's rule and reign over all creation that has been lost through our sin. That restoration has already begun in the perfect King, Jesus, who now reigns from His heavenly throne and will return to reign forever as King of a new heaven and new earth. But the Kingdom is more than that.

The Kingdom of Heaven is the ultimate answer to the question, Why is there still evil and suffering in the world? The Kingdom will right all wrongs at the right time. It is not yet, but it is here now. It is future, but it is present. Even a young child knows that the world is not right, that there is terrible suffering, oppression, poverty, and injustice. When you form your children's imaginations, you are enabling them to see the Kingdom as God's response to all that is not right in the world. You are enabling them to see that they, too, as members of that Kingdom, have a part to play in God's Kingdom story—faithfully serving in Christ's name by declaring the Good News of salvation in Him, offering the cup of cold water in His name, and helping to ease the pain, injustice, and suffering of others. Their role is to love God with all they are and to love others with all Jesus is. That's what they can do, because that's what Jesus came to do (see Matthew 5–7). Imagine that!

Sally's Lifegiving Momoirs

Sarah was always our "book girl." She started reading on her own at five and had read all of The Chronicles of Narnia, the Little House series, and many other books by the time she was seven. She was the girl who won library contests for the number of books read in a summer. She loved books and reading from the time she could turn a page, and she still does.

During the six years we lived in Texas, Sarah had many good friends. But when she was fourteen we moved to Monument, Colorado, and she had no friends there. It was a lonely time for her at an age when girlfriends are an important part of growing up. She had read all of the Anne of Green Gables books when she was younger, but now that she was a teen like Anne, she revisited the series. She also read about the author, Lucy Maud Montgomery, and how her imagined stories about Anne Shirley and Diana Barry had been inspired by her own life experiences. Sarah would sit on a boulder on the hill behind our Colorado home to read. She dreamed of becoming a writer like Lucy Maud Montgomery, whose stories about the kinds of girlfriends Sarah didn't have then encouraged her and fed her imagination.

Sarah wanted to tell stories that would capture imaginations in the same way. What she couldn't see then is that this period of loneliness would create strategic and undistracted time for her to think about stories and writing, and even to take her first steps into a life of writing. Just two years later, at sixteen, she had completed her homeschooling senior project, *Journeys of Faithfulness: Stories for the Heart for Faithful Girls*, an imaginative retelling of the stories of four single women in the Bible in a two-hundred-page illustrated book. She would later write a book titled *Read for the Heart*, about books and reading for children, and *Caught Up in a Story*, which focuses on the power of story in children's lives. She will soon write a book about books for women, and she is working on a fiction novella. When I look back and think how sad I was to see my fourteen-year-old daughter alone without friends in those years, I'm also reminded that imagination needs time and space to grow. By God's grace, those lonely years allowed the heart of a budding writer the time to find her imagination and later release it as an author who will influence many through her words and stories.

Lifegiving ParenTips

The cost of imagination. In the early days of our parenting, Sally and I read an article that suggested the best way to invest in our children's futures was by investing in tools they might later use for vocation and ministry. That principle made sense to us, and we started a habit of devoting resources to our children's skills, abilities, and to some degree their imaginations—what they dreamed they might do someday. Rather than withholding these tools until a birthday or Christmas or making the children earn them, we simply gave them to our children when it seemed appropriate to encourage a budding interest or pursuit—books, electronics, instruments, software, sports gear, science equipment, and other such things. Some might wonder if our children were spoiled or if some things went unused. No, they were not spoiled. Yes, some things weren't used, but they were still good investments in our children. We gave things without strings as we were able. It will cost you more money, but as your financial situation allows, be prepared to invest generously in your children's lives and imaginations.

The cost of a "different" child. Many families have a mysterious or "different" child who often has an exceptionally active imagination and can be creative in nontraditional ways. Nathan was our different child. We didn't know about his ADD and OCD until his midteens, so during childhood we just thought he was a challenging boy with a very strong, extroverted personality. There was a mysterious part of him we accepted but didn't understand. We paid in a lot of investment in faith and patience during Nathan's childhood and exponentially more during his young adulthood. But we never gave up on him, forced him to be something he was not, or tried to put labels on him. We hung in with him and did all we could to affirm his aspirations to be an actor. Now as an adult, he has written, acted in, and produced two feature-length films. We were able to be a part of seeing him grow and develop and spread the Kingdom of God through his creative skills. If you have a "different" child, you will experience a cost, but you will also experience rewards as your child's imagination helps them find a different path to life with God.

Imaginal parenting. If you're going to form your children's imaginations, you need to be feeding your own. Every personality type has an imagination that needs to be used, lest it starve and atrophy. It won't do to say, "I'm just not the creative type." For the sake of your children, who will be watching to see how you use your imagination, take some time every week to foster it. Read a work of fiction or fantasy. Listen to new or different music. Try writing a poem, song, short story, liturgical prayer, or psalm. Slowly appreciate a book of art by a favorite painter. Imagine what you would do if you could do anything, and write it down to share with your kids. If you're artistic, think about creating a series of drawings or paintings about faith, hope, and love; if you're not artistic, try your hand at some creative renderings of Bible verses with "illuminations." Use your imagination! Your children will approve.

Starting the Heartbeat of Parental Lifegiving

Forming your child's imagination starts with the image of God, which draws us into relationship with Him and enables our imaginations. Imagining is a mental faculty that you as a parent can help to form, and one by which, in part, your children will believe in the God of the Bible, whom they cannot see or touch.

PART II

Living as a Lifegiving Parent

CHAPTER 10

ONE LIFE TO GIVE

We will not hide these truths from our children; we will tell the next generation about the glorious deeds of the LORD, about his power and his mighty wonders.

PSALM 78:4, NLT

EVERY GENERATION seems to find a rallying motto. Some, like the recent "YOLO" (You Only Live Once), flash briefly only to be corrupted and discarded. Others, like the 1989 generational motto "Carpe diem!" ("Seize the day!") popularized in the movie *Dead Poets Society*, are still celebrated decades later. The ancient Latin aphorism, declared by the English-teacher character portrayed by Robin Williams, captured the imaginations and spirits of a new generation. It also captures the "One Life to Give" attitude for lifegiving parenting that we'll discuss in this chapter. As a parent, you have a limited opportunity to give your children a life worth living for Christ—one window of time to give to them from your life what God has designed them to receive from His. So seize the days!

In this final chapter we come full circle, looking back to the first chapter of the book, where we considered the Shema of Israel. More than any other words written by Moses, the Shema would define the new nation of Israel: "Hear, O Israel! The LORD is our God, the LORD is one! You shall love the LORD your God with all your heart and with all your soul and with all your might" (Deuteronomy 6:4-5). The phrase "Shema Yisra'el" (Hear, O Israel) was certainly the "Carpe diem!" for the Israelites of that day, and it continues to be for many Jews today, 3,500 years later. But Moses went on to apply the Shema to the parents of Israel. They were to teach their children God's truth diligently, at home and on the road, during all their waking hours, with everything in their lives. It was Moses' way of saying, "You have only one life to give your children all of God that they need. Seize their days!"

But now we're going to move that story forward. Though Israel is looking across the Jordan at the Promised Land, God does not allow Moses to enter, and the patriarch dies there at age 120. General Joshua, appointed by Moses to be his successor, takes on the mantle of leadership and prepares to conquer and occupy the land of Canaan that God had promised to Abraham five hundred years earlier. God confirms Joshua's leadership by holding back the waters of the Jordan River in the same way He had parted the Red Sea for Moses years before. The people of Israel cross on dry ground again, this time into the new land. Before the priests carrying the Ark of the Covenant come up from the dry riverbed, allowing the Jordan's water to return to its banks, God directs Joshua to appoint one man from each of the twelve tribes of Israel to pick up a large stone from the middle of the Jordan and carry it to the new encampment at Gilgal. There the twelve stones are set up as a memorial to God. That evening, their first night in the Promised Land, Joshua addresses the people.

As a military man, Joshua makes his words few but to the point. Just as Moses directed the Shema to the parents of Israel concerning the Law that God was giving them, so also Joshua directs his words to the parents of Israel concerning the land that God is giving them. "When your children ask their fathers in time to come, saying, 'What are these stones?' then you shall inform your children, saying, 'Israel crossed this Jordan on dry ground'" (Joshua 4:21-22). He goes on to tell them the purpose of the miracle, "that all the peoples of the earth may know that the hand of the LORD is mighty, so that you may fear the LORD your God forever" (v. 24). This is what they are to tell their children—that the LORD, the God of Israel who dried up the waters of the Jordan to bring them into the Promised Land, is faithful, sovereign, and mighty in the earth and is to be reverently feared all their days.

The parents of Israel have been charged twice now, first by Moses and then by Joshua, about their importance to the future of their nation. You'd think they would get the message, but the rest of the story says otherwise. Joshua proceeds to lead a successful military campaign to conquer the land of Canaan for the new nation of Israel. The people will need to settle the land they now occupy without compromising with the pagan populations still living there. When the land is at rest and Joshua is ready to retire, he gathers all Israel and its leaders together at Shechem for a last speech.

Joshua charges Israel to fear the Lord, serve Him sincerely, and renounce any other gods they had once served. He makes clear his own family's choice: "If it is disagreeable in your sight to serve the LORD, choose for yourselves today whom you will serve . . . but as for me and my house, we will serve the LORD" (Joshua 24:15). In a covenant ceremony of call and response, Joshua then challenges the people of Israel to remain faithful to the Lord, warning them of God's judgment if they forsake Him. But the people reply, "We will serve the LORD our God and we will obey His voice" (v. 24). The covenant is sealed with a stone memorial, all are dismissed to their inheritances, and Joshua dies at age 110.

The unraveling doesn't take long. "All [Joshua's] generation also were gathered to their fathers; and there arose another generation after them who did not know the LORD, nor yet the work which He had done for Israel. Then the sons of Israel did evil in the sight of the LORD and served the Baals, and they forsook the LORD, the God of their fathers . . . thus they provoked the LORD to anger" (Judges 2:10-12). Faithfulness died in one generation. Just one. And notice who is included in that unfaithful generation—the children of those parents who had heard the words of both Moses and Joshua. Their parents apparently neither diligently taught them the Law nor told them how God, the LORD, brought Israel into the land. They didn't help their children remember who God is and what He had done. Those children were the ones who did evil and forsook the Lord.

⸙ ⸙

The story sounds like it must have happened over a relatively long period of time. But listen again—it all happened in only about thirty years. Let that sink in. It took very little time within the context of Israel's history for those children to forget God. That should be a sober reminder to us as parents that we, too, have our children for a very brief time to prepare them to live for God as adults. The parents of Israel who lived after Joshua did not do so well; that should not be our story.

The account of this brief window of time in the story of Israel changed our lives as a couple. It is the root of the concept of life-giving parenting presented in this book. It is certainly the root of one of the most lifegiving traditions Sally and I started as a newly married couple in 1981 and have continued every year since—first as a couple, and then as a family. During our first year of marriage, while I was teaching a three-month series on the book of Joshua for our little church in Littleton, Colorado, the story of the memorial stones caught our imaginations. We decided we would choose a new verse for our marriage each year on our anniversary, and a "memorial stone" to commemorate it, typically a small piece of artwork. In 1990, with three children ages six and under, we realized it was time to make the memorial stones a family matter. We held our first official "Family Day" on the Saturday of Labor Day weekend, close to our August 30 anniversary. I think that first year we tried to write on real stones—twelve smooth river rocks. Not a good idea. The next year we tried something new that worked much better, and still does.

For our 1991 Family Day, we gathered the children and told them we wanted to recall all the ways that God had been faithful to us as a family in the year before, and then to make some memorial stones. Testimonials of God's faithfulness came readily from the mouths of our young ones—how God gave us a new home, provided new friends, gave us a dog, and other childlike affirmations. I wrote them all down, assigned each item on the list to a family member, and handed out sheets of colored paper. The children then used markers, pens, pencils, and crayons to illustrate as best as they could the items of God's faithfulness assigned to them. Those drawings were our memorial stones and would go, with the list, into a Family Day binder. Over the years we got a bit more sophisticated with special printouts for the lists and artwork, but other than adding prayer requests for the year ahead, nothing has changed since 1991.

As I write this, we're about to celebrate our twenty-seventh Family Day. By God's grace, we've never had a Family Day without every child at home. We'll start the day with a breakfast of homemade cinnamon rolls and hot chocolate. Then we'll spend the morning reviewing the previous year's memorial stones, sharing faithfulness testimonials of the past year, making new memorial stone drawings, and choosing a Bible verse and sharing prayer requests for the year ahead. Around noon, we'll head up to the mountains for a picnic lunch of Sally's pan-fried chicken tenders, baked beans, and chocolate sheet cake. We'll hike a favorite trail, have a lot of fun with each other, and take a copious number of family and individual photos. On the way back down from the mountains, we'll stop for coffee and conversation.

We have Joshua to thank for this wonderful day to be our family and mark the years together, but our Family Day is more than just a fun tradition. It's a lifegiving anchor—perhaps the most lifegiving thing we do during the year for our children. Why? Because it allows them to see God's hand in and on the Clarksons—that He is alive in our family, that His life intersects our lives in real and tangible ways, and that He never stops being faithful to us. Year after year our children acknowledge God's presence in our lives, and over the years they see the pattern of God's continuing faithfulness to us. We can all agree together with the apostle Paul, "Faithful is He who calls you, and He also will bring it to pass" (1 Thessalonians 5:24). Whether you're just starting your family or you're a ways down the family road, it's never too late to pick a time and start to celebrate your own Family Day. Whether you model your day after ours or come up with your own creative approach, the key is to make it a regular, dedicated time to remember God's faithfulness to your family.

❧　☙

Memorial stones seemed like such a great idea for Israel, but everything went south after Joshua died. The unfaithful Israelites became dysfunctional and disjointed, going through recurring cycles of apostasy, oppression by enemies, and cries of distress to God, who then gave them judges "who delivered them from the hands of those who plundered them" (Judges 2:16). It was an age in which "there was no king in Israel; everyone did what was right in his own eyes" (21:25). But then, after about three centuries of failure, God acceded to the Israelites' demands and gave them kings like the nations around them—Saul, whose heart was not God's; David, whose heart was fully God's; and Solomon, whose heart was half God's. It was during this time of stability that David and others wrote most of the Psalms of Israel, the poetic expressions of worship that would define the ideal heart of the nation.

Asaph was one of David's leading musicians in the Tabernacle during that time, a worship leader of the people and a personal prophet to David through his music. Twelve of his songs are included in the Psalter. In Psalm 78, Asaph tells the story of Israel's often wayward history, concluding with David as God's trusted and skilled shepherd of the people. In the preamble (vv. 1-8) to the long psalm, though, he hearkens back to the words of Moses and Joshua, reaffirming that the future of Israel is in the hands of its parents.

Asaph declares that the people have heard the stories of Israel from their fathers, and they "will not conceal them from their children, but tell to the generation to come the praises of the LORD, and His strength and His wondrous works that He has done" (v. 4). One hears echoes of Joshua in these opening words, and then of Moses as Asaph goes on to say their fathers were given the stories and the Law along with a command from God: "That they should teach them to their children, that the generation to come might know, even the children yet to be born, that they may arise and tell them to their children" (vv. 5-6). Then he reaffirms the critical role of parents in the future of Israel: "That [the children of future generations] should put their confidence in God and not forget the works of God, but keep His commandments" (v. 7). He closes with a warning, like Joshua's, that they should not be like their fathers' generation "that did not prepare its heart and whose spirit was not faithful to God" (v. 8).

It's easy, from the perspective of our modern culture, to minimize the words of Moses and Joshua, and even Asaph—a few dozen words in the midst of thousands, by patriarchs of an ancient nomadic tribal culture, recorded in Scripture some three millennia ago. But time and truth have not dismissed their words, so neither should we. And we can also add words spoken by God about Abraham: "I have chosen him, so that he may command his children and his household after him to keep the way of the LORD by doing righteousness and justice, so that the LORD may bring upon Abraham what He has spoken about him" (Genesis 18:19)—the birth of a great nation by which "all the families of the earth will be blessed" (12:2-3). At the critical points in the story of Israel, God fulfills His promises, announcing a people through Abraham, a law through Moses, and a land through Joshua. These three—a people, a law, and a land—will define Israel as a nation, and as each is given, God also declares that family and parenting will be at the heart of His plans for Israel.

The principles of parenting that God painted into the portrait of Israel are no less true for us today; God has been painting them into the pictures of every generation of His people for as long as He has revealed His will to us through His inspired holy writings. The theme of family is certainly continued in the New Testament and given new meaning in Christ—that believers are children of God (John 1:12), adopted into His eternal family (Ephesians 1:5), and given a dwelling place in the Father's house (John 14:2). When Paul instructed the Ephesians about family, he drew on the fifth commandment to encourage children to obey their parents (6:1-3) and then reflected the words of the Shema when he admonished fathers to "bring them up in the discipline and instruction of the Lord" (v. 4). God's principles of parenting never change.

After all that biblical history, here's the take-home (literally): Good and godly parenting is a critical key to the work of God in the world. Of course, it is the Holy Spirit in the people of God doing the eternal work of redemption—building Christ's church, preserving God's Word, extending the Kingdom. But the continued story of the church also depends on us, as parents after God's heart, telling our children the stories of His faithfulness and teaching them the blessings of His truth so that they will tell their children and their children's children about "the excellencies of Him who has called you out of darkness into His marvelous light" (1 Peter 2:9). That is what Asaph was reminding God's people of in his day; that is what the Holy Spirit is reminding God's people of in our day. That is what I mean by the chapter title "One Life to Give"—we each have only one life, not just to live, but also to give to our children. There's only one way to be a truly lifegiving parent—by giving our children the life of God.

※ ※

There is no secret formula for becoming a lifegiving parent. I hope that's clear from the eight heartbeats of lifegiving parenting we've explored together. Lifegiving is all about . . . life! It's not a program, curriculum, or set of procedures that you can follow and be done with. It's life, and life is both always being done and never done. Lifegiving parenting is organic, natural, relational, and it can even be impromptu and a bit messy. It's a mental and spiritual attitude about and toward your children. It may sound cliché to say, but lifegiving parenting is not just about what you do but is mostly about who you are. By that I mean it's not what you do that defines who you are, but who you are that defines what you do. That's why the starting place to becoming a lifegiving parent is about determining to *know* the right things that will keep you on the right path—to know yourself as a parent, your children as good, your God as faithful, and your times as God's.

If you get a handle on these four critical priorities of your parenting life, and you get a grip on what giving life to your children is really about, then lifegiving parenting will take care of itself. You'll see the life of God abounding in your home, and your children will see it too. Over time, God will become more than just a Sunday school lesson or a Bible story; He'll be the living God living with you.

Before we turn the page for one final story about Israel, I want to look briefly at each of these four priorities of things you need to know. Use these brief explorations as opportunities for self-evaluation and planning. They will help you see yourself in the final picture of Israel we'll look at as we end the chapter.

Know Yourself as a Parent

Every Christian parent knows Solomon's pithy proverb "Train up a child in the way he should go, even when he is old he will not depart from it" (Proverbs 22:6). But let me reimagine that verse as written about parents: "Train up parents in the way they should go; even as they get older they will not depart from it." Look around and you can find moms and dads who want to be good parents but don't seem to be prepared for the task. They have picked up proverbs, opinions, and maxims along the way, and they do whatever seems to work or whatever their friends are doing, but you can sense there's something missing. You, though, have the opportunity to be a "trained up" parent for the sake of your children, to take them with you on the way you all should go with God. It doesn't mean you'll know everything there is to know about God's plan for parenting, or even that you'll always get it right, but you'll be learning from God what it means to be a parent for Him while following His lead.

The first step to knowing yourself as that kind of parent, though, is to know yourself as a person. Becoming a biological parent does not bring with it a mysterious mantle of maturity that fills you with wisdom and discernment. Godly parenting is a learned task, not just from books and talks but also from real-life experience and sharing the journey with other Christian parents. But being trained up as a parent also means understanding the person inside you, your humanity, and that is much more an internal and spiritual journey toward maturity in Christ.

We've all said it at one time or another: "Well, I am just human." We might laugh as we excuse some commonly shared fault, but behind the smile we might also feel embarrassment, shame, or guilt. Being "just human" can be downright humbling, and that's never truer than when it involves our children. We all know the parental fumbles and foibles that pull back the curtain to reveal our imperfect humanity—the harsh correction, the out-of-control toddler, the too-tired-to-intervene sibling spat, and so many more.

We don't need to be reminded that we're all sinful. It comes with the territory of being human, and especially with being a parent. But we can let our sinfulness obscure some other important truths that should affect our parenting even more. We're made in God's image, so we're connected to His life (see Genesis 1:26-27). Scripture also says we are made "only a little lower than God and crowned . . . with glory and honor" (Psalm 8:5, NLT). And Jesus reminds us many times that we are loved, enough that He would die for us (see John 3:16). Here's what we need to know about ourselves as parents following after God's heart: We are very special, deeply fallen, and greatly loved. That is what it means to be human in God's eyes.

Even with those affirming six words about our humanity in our minds, though, we still might feel that we need to be in control of our parenting to please God. Whether or not that's a realistic goal we could ever reach, the real issue is not if we're in control but rather what's in control of us. We humans are complex creatures, shaped internally by drives, fears, pride, ideals, hopes, and other unseen but influential forces. We won't fully understand our parenting until we can get a grip on how those forces control who we are and how we think and act. Even though they are not likely to be completely "in control" of you, let me suggest just a few representative negative influences that could affect your parenting.

When the sinful self, often called "the flesh," is in control, we're not thinking about God or doing His will. Even though we are new creatures in Christ, we are still tempted by our sinful nature. And if we let emotions control us, strong feelings can affect how we interact with our immature children. Emotion-filled reactions such as anger, judgment, or criticism can replace thoughtful and reasoned actions. Also, we can let fear—of what others think, of doing the wrong thing, of angering God—control us. Fear can prevent us from trusting God and relating in a healthy way with our children. Finally, there is formula and habit—uncritically following patterns we've been told are the best methods of parenting or just parenting thoughtlessly by habits and routines.

Those negative human forces, and many more, can influence our parenting, but only if we let them. The good news is that we have a choice; we can learn to let God be in control of our parenting. We can let Him become the controlling influence in our lives so our children will see the new persons we are becoming in Christ, not the old persons we were before. That happens through three positive influences by which God comes into our humanity—faith, freedom, and love. Much of parenting is simply learning to "walk by faith, not by sight" (2 Corinthians 5:7)—trusting in God for His wisdom, insight, and discernment to become the Christlike parents our children need. Faith, then, gives us the freedom to follow the Holy Spirit's ministry in our hearts and not be enslaved to man's laws and rules. "It was for freedom that Christ set us free" (Galatians 5:1), so we are fulfilling His greatest purpose in our lives when we listen to His Spirit. Freedom, then, enables us to love as Christ loved us. When we are motivated by love, we fulfill God's expectations of us as people and as parents through the power of Christ's Spirit within us (see Galatians 5:22-23). Love is the ultimate virtue by which we can become godly parents.

Maybe you're remembering right now the words of Jesus—"You are to be perfect, as your heavenly Father is perfect" (Matthew 5:48). Since we are all imperfect Christian parents, that verse can give one pause. But the Greek word for "perfect," *teleios*, can also refer to "completeness" or "wholeness." So take Jesus' words as an encouragement—He wants you to find your wholeness as a person, who also happens to be a parent, in Him. That's what He sent His Holy Spirit to do in our lives: to make us—as sinful, fragmented humans—whole in Him. That wholehearted person is who you can become as a parent and the person your children will love to know. Just remember: As a parent, you are very special, deeply fallen, and greatly loved. And so are your children, so show them as their parent what that means.

Know Your Child as Good

Of all that gets said in this book, I hope this is one idea that sticks: Be your children's advocate, not their adversary. Too many parents can become de facto sin police, ready to punish any violation lest their children become unrepentant rebels. Of course you need to correct your children's incorrect behaviors, but how you perceive yourself in that responsibility will determine whether you bend their wills to yours or draw their hearts to yours. You have an opportunity to be your children's advocate, just as Jesus is for us: "My little children, I am writing these things to you so that you may not sin. And if anyone sins, we have an Advocate with the Father, Jesus Christ the righteous" (1 John 2:1). Rather than a behavior cop, you can be a heart counsel. Rather than an adversary assuming you'll catch your children doing bad, you can become an advocate expecting to find them doing good. That is a lifegiving attitude.

Childhood is a specific stage of life during which, by God's design, you have open access to your child's heart. John addresses the recipients of his first letter as "little children," "young men," and "fathers" (1 John 2:12-14). The "children" he mentions were certainly adult followers of Jesus, but his words reinforce the idea, expressed or suggested in other passages throughout Scripture, that the natural three-stage pattern of human development is that childhood is preparation for young adulthood, which is preparation for adulthood. Childhood in Scripture is considered a time of innocence (see Deuteronomy 1:39; 2 Samuel 12:21-23; Hebrews 5:13-14) prior to the time when a child will begin to choose between good and evil. As we considered in chapter 8 in the parable of the Sower and in the life of Timothy, a young child can have an "honest and good heart" (Luke 8:15) that is able to value the goodness of God.

Paul also spoke of children: "When I was a child, I used to speak like a child, think like a child, reason like a child; when I became a man, I did away with childish things" (1 Corinthians 13:11). You may be conditioned to hear those words as pejorative, but Paul was simply recognizing, like John, that childhood is a divinely designed stage of development toward maturity—it is as God intends it to be. Paul said much the same thing in Ephesians, contrasting becoming a "mature man" with "we are no longer to be children" (4:13-14). Advocate parents recognize that children are immature and developing, and that is as it should be. They see the goodness of God's design in that immaturity, not just the badness of sin. An advocate parent responds to and gives life where life is growing.

Know Your God as Faithful

No matter how lifegiving any parent tries to be, at times we all become lifetaking. Not in the literal sense, of course, but in the sense of draining life out of our children rather than filling them up. Whether with words of anger, disappointment, guilt, or shame, we say things that tear our children down rather than build them up. Paul warned the fathers at the church in Colossae, "Do not exasperate your children, so that they will not lose heart" (Colossians 3:21). We all can, and do, give in to our sinful natures. However, though we don't "lose heart" when our children sin against us, our children do when we sin against them—we provoke them to anger or stir up their passions, which leaves them broken in spirit or, literally, without passions. Breaking our children's spirits is not the way to win their hearts.

Thank goodness for Paul's encouragement about God's faithfulness in his last letter to Timothy: "If we are faithless, He remains faithful, for He cannot deny Himself" (2 Timothy 2:13). Even when we go off the rails of our intentions to be faithful parents, God doesn't change. He remains faithful to who He is and, if we are His, to us. Moses affirmed it when he gave the Shema to Israel: "The LORD your God, He is God, the faithful God" (Deuteronomy 7:9). Jeremiah affirmed it: "Because of the LORD's great love we are not consumed, for his compassions never fail. They are new every morning; great is your faithfulness" (Lamentations 3:22-23, NIV). Paul affirmed it: "The Lord is faithful, and He will strengthen and protect you from the evil one" (2 Thessalonians 3:3). Despite whatever unfaithfulness you may see in yourself as a lifegiving parent, God is a faithful Father—the ultimate lifegiving parent—and He will remain faithful to you.

If you want to be a faithful and lifegiving parent, know that your God is faithful. Here's a verse to keep in mind: "Without faith it is impossible to please Him, for he who comes to God must believe that He is and that He is a rewarder of those who seek Him" (Hebrews 11:6). Let me break that down to some simpler terms for this priority: Have faith, faithfully trust God, trust in God's faithfulness. The priority to know your God as faithful is an anchor—it will keep you from drifting away from being the lifegiving parent you want to be.

Know Your Times as God's

This last priority is about keeping an attitude of trust in God, no matter what your times as a parent may hold. David did this through his difficulties: "As for me, I trust in You, O LORD, I say, 'You are my God.' *My times are in Your hand*" (Psalm 31:14-15, emphasis added). David repeatedly called God his rock, refuge, and strength, "a very present help in trouble" (46:1). Perhaps that trust is what prompted his son Solomon's words: "So that your trust may be in the LORD, I have taught you today, even you" (Proverbs 22:19). The truth is that your times—the details of your life and the circumstances of your parenting—really are in God's hand. Knowing that will make your lifegiving parenting relevant no matter what is happening. Your times are God's times.

Knowing that your times are God's, though, is not the same as knowing the times you live in. Remember Paul's admonition in Romans 12:2: "Do not be conformed to this world [age], but be transformed by the renewing of your mind." Don't allow your mind to be influenced by your own culture's ways of thinking. Stop letting the isms of your day become the ways you think about God, life, and even your children. It's not enough just to know your times are God's; you have to learn how to live in God's time.

We are bound by Providence to the particular slice of history, and His story, in which we find ourselves as parents. We cannot be parents in first-century Jerusalem, or in sixteenth-century Europe, or in Victorian England. It is our particular calling to be Christian parents in twenty-first-century America, or wherever you are reading this book. The times and locations in which we live will shape how we know ourselves as parents, how we know our children as good, and how we know our God as faithful. By faith, we accept the call to be godly parents where we are and say with Joshua, "As for me and my house, we will serve the LORD" (Joshua 24:15).

⚜ ⚜

Let's turn the page now on that final story about Israel. The glory days of Israel's history under Saul, David, and Solomon are short lived. The wheels come off that golden chariot in 931 BC when Solomon dies and his son Rehoboam causes the division of the land—ten tribes in the northern kingdom of Israel; two tribes in the southern kingdom of Judah. Just 209 years later in 722 BC, Assyria conquers the northern kingdom. In 586 BC, Babylon conquers the southern kingdom and takes many of the remaining Israelites into exile.

But let's focus on just the last seventy-six years of Judah's history before the exile. Beginning with Rehoboam, fifteen kings rule in Jerusalem with varying degrees of integrity and skill, mostly with little of either. Over that period of nearly three hundred years, pagan worship and idolatry spread unchecked, the Law is forgotten, and the Temple in Jerusalem falls into disrepair and corruption. Josiah is eight years old when he becomes king of Israel in 640 BC, following fifty-seven years of wicked rule by his father and brother. At sixteen, Josiah begins "to seek the God of his father David" (2 Chronicles 34:3). At twenty, he cleanses all the land of pagan altars and idols. At twenty-six, he begins to restore the Temple and discovers the forgotten Law of God in the rubble. As it is read aloud, he is deeply convicted and seeks the Lord. His repentance begins a revival in Judah for the remaining twelve years of his reign.

Now imagine among the nobles in Josiah's courts is a young couple who responds to his call for repentance and obedience out of their love for God. And imagine that couple has a child and raises him during the revival. When their child is about twelve years old in 609 BC, Josiah dies. Suspecting that Judah's days are few, the child's parents begin to train their son in all the Law and ways of the Lord, pouring their hearts into him. Just four years later, in 605 BC, King Nebuchadnezzar of Babylon enters Jerusalem, raids the Temple, and deports the best and the brightest of the young Israelite nobles back to Babylon. Among them is a handsome young man, now around the age of sixteen, named . . . Daniel.

You know the rest of his story. Like Josiah at sixteen in Judah, Daniel at sixteen in Babylon takes a stand for the God of Israel. Over his lifetime in exile he distinguishes himself before Kings Nebuchadnezzar and Cyrus and the people of Babylon, becoming a faithful witness for "the Most High God [who] is ruler over the realm of mankind" (Daniel 5:21). His faithfulness is a testimony to the people of Israel in captivity, encouraging them to remain faithful, preserve the Law, and prepare to return after seventy years of exile to rebuild Jerusalem and the Temple.

If such an account might be true, Daniel was raised by parents who showed him the living God. In refusing the king's food, being cast into the lions' den, and interpreting dreams before King Nebuchadnezzar at risk of his life, Daniel was confident that the living God was with him. I like to think that Daniel's parents knew they had one life to give, and they poured it into him. They were lifegiving parents.

⁓   ⁓

Most of us live as though we know what the future holds—life will go on, and as our children count on a certain amount of predictability, we as parents will share the journey with them until God calls us home to be with Him. While all that may be true, the words of James remind us not to become too comfortable with our assumptions: "You do not even know what will happen tomorrow. What is your life? You are a mist that appears for a little while and then vanishes" (James 4:14, NIV). Some might hear fatalism in those words, but if you're a parent with a lifegiving heart, you should hear a challenge. If James's words are a call, then Psalm 90:12 is the response: "So teach us to number our days, that we may present to You a heart of wisdom." That's why we number our children's days and then continue to live to the rhythm of the other heartbeats of lifegiving parenting. Whatever the future may hold, we want to face it knowing we did all we could to give our children the life of God.

There's no way for you to know if the children you're raising will become Daniels in their generation. All you can know is that you're doing all you can to prepare them, if that is what God asks of them. Regardless of where or when you start that preparation, you can give your sons and daughters the life of God they'll need to choose to be a Daniel. You can be the kind of lifegiving parent who gives your children whatever they need to be faithful followers of God in whatever situations life gives to them. It's simply about choosing to invest your "one life to give" into the hearts of your children. If that's what you do, then you'll be a lifegiving parent, and the living God will be alive in your life—and in your children's lives.

OUR LIFEGIVING PARENT STORY

I have no greater joy than this, to hear of my children walking in the truth.

3 JOHN 1:4

SALLY AND I STILL HAVE the memorial stone we chose together for our first year of marriage. Our verse was a familiar one from Jesus' Sermon on the Mount. It actually pulled double duty, serving as a lifetime marriage verse in addition to a first-year memorial stone verse, and it has held up to that task.

It's in the passage where Jesus tells His followers, "Do not be worried about your life, as to what you will eat or what you will drink; nor for your body, as to what you will put on. Is not life more than food, and the body more than clothing?" (Matthew 6:25). He makes the point that worry is a waste of time that stems from a lack of faith, so there's no reason for those who love Him to worry like nonbelievers, who seek so intently after temporary things like food and clothing. Instead, Jesus says, "Your heavenly Father knows that you need all these things. But seek first His kingdom and His righteousness, and all these things will be added to you" (vv. 32-33).

In simplest terms, seeking God's Kingdom means not seeking and trusting in kingdoms and things of this world but seeking and trusting in the King of kings, who now rules from heaven and will one day rule on earth. At its heart, seeking God's Kingdom is an act of allegiance.

Jesus used the flowers of the field as an illustration of God's care for His children, so our memorial stone that first year was a simple arrangement of dried wildflowers pressed between two pieces of glass in a minimalist standing brass frame. Our verse was Matthew 6:33, mostly the "seek first His kingdom" part, which called us as a couple to live for Christ in all we did. On another level, the "all these things will be added" part was also a reminder as we were starting out as a couple to "not worry about tomorrow; for tomorrow will care for itself. Each day has enough trouble of its own" (v. 34). Both parts have proved to be true of our married and family life for thirty-six years. Maybe a bit too true at times.

We kept seeking first the Kingdom of God as children filled up our lives and home, but we began to notice a change in our perspectives—a conviction that crept into our lives and gradually took over. Before kids, our focus on the Kingdom was always "out there" in the world, spreading the Kingdom through ministry. After kids, our focus on the Kingdom became more and more "in here" in our home, building the Kingdom in our family. We began seeking the Kingdom in our children's hearts—they became our first priority. We still were seeking the Kingdom in our ministry to parents and families, but it was never to the exclusion of our children. In fact, we included them in our ministries. We knew that if we didn't reach their hearts with a Kingdom vision and understanding of life, then all our other ministry would seem empty and meaningless by comparison.

Our children are now grown, and we can say with confidence that all of them are walking with God and seeking His Kingdom and righteousness in their lives. This book is about our journey of parenting and what we learned through it about being lifegiving parents, so it's primarily about our story. However, since our children were obviously the point of all our parenting (there are no stories without them), it would seem somehow incomplete if we didn't at the very least let you know where they are now and how they've turned out. We simply want to introduce you to the objects of our lifegiving parenting and weave a little bit more of the colors of their current lives into the story that is the tapestry of the Clarkson family. They are, after all, the ultimate expressions of that first memorial stone and marriage verse that set us on the path of the Kingdom as a couple and as parents. Meet our lifegiven children: Sarah, Joel, Nathan, and Joy.

⤙ ⤚

Sarah, thirty-four, is married and living in Oxford, England. Her husband, Thomas, from the Netherlands, is studying at Oxford University and training for the Anglican priesthood. Sarah is a prolific reader, driven by her intuitive insights about life to quietly influence others to know the God of creation, who is her inspiration. Her home is a place of beauty where she and Thomas minister to others and where their children will find the life of God in all its goodness and truth. She wanted from a young age to become a writer and now uses her gift with words to challenge, encourage, and inspire others to seek God and His Kingdom. She wants to explore subjects such as beauty, imagination, and suffering. In addition to writing three books for Christian families, Sarah cowrote *The Lifegiving Home* with Sally, and she is currently writing a new book for Tyndale— *Book Girl*, an invitation to the reading life for Christian women. She completed her bachelor of theology from Oxford in 2017. Sarah is a Reflective Mover.[1]

Joel, thirty-one, is a writer, thinker, and musician in the courts of God's Kingdom. He was musical from an early age, and he graduated with a degree in composition in 2011 from Berklee College of Music. He wants to use his postcollege experience in orchestration and choral composition to strengthen the church and help others appreciate the aesthetics of worship, especially in liturgical and sacramental traditions. Joel is an author and essayist, writing on topics ranging from theology and worship to finding a richer and more meaningful life of Christian faith and devotion. He is a natural instructor who is driven to help others understand biblical concepts. He and our daughter Joy record and perform their original songs as the duet Two Benedictions. Joel cowrote the study guides for *The Lifegiving Home, The Lifegiving Table*, and *Different*. He is studying at the University of St. Andrews in Scotland, pursuing a graduate degree in theology, imagination, and the arts. Joel is both a Reflective and an Active Mover.

Nathan, twenty-nine, has always been an independent dream chaser in the family. He was our challenging child growing up, which we came to realize was the result of his struggles with obsessive-compulsive disorder (OCD), attention deficit disorder (ADD), and learning disabilities. He and Sally wrote about their experiences from both sides of the parent-child relationship in their Tyndale book *Different*. He is driven by his natural extroversion, biblical convictions, and intuitive grasp of ideas to think of new ways to challenge Christians to a deeper faith and a Kingdom mentality. He has wanted to be an actor since his teens, and has written, acted in, and produced two feature-length faith-based films: *Confessions of a Prodigal Son* and *The Not So Good Samaritan*. He has written books on the Christian life for young men and always has creative projects in process. He studied acting and has lived both in New York City and Los Angeles, looking for ways to be a lifegiving light for Christ to other actors. Nathan is an Active Shaper.

Joy, twenty-three, is always engaging with people. From a young age, she has been a natural Christian leader, influencing and encouraging others with her winsome personality and lifegiving insights.

Her heart for God as a young woman shapes her future hopes and plans as she explores how to invest her gifts for God's Kingdom. She is a natural thinker and debater, having won national awards in speech and debate while at Biola University. Joy is also an aspiring Christian writer and author. She contributed to a study guide for one of Sally's books, was a cowriter for *The Lifegiving Table* study guide, and wrote a one-act play performed at a national cultural event in England. She also loves songwriting and singing and records and performs with Joel as Two Benedictions. She earned a graduate degree in theology, imagination, and the arts in 2017 from the University of St. Andrews in Scotland and is now pursuing her doctorate there in the same program. Joy is an Active Mover.

❦ ❧

That was just a very quick glance at the four wonderful people God allowed us as parents to shepherd into adulthood. Our goals were always, and only, about raising good and godly children to become wholehearted adults who would follow Christ and seek God's Kingdom. In our education, training, and discipleship of our children through childhood and young adulthood, we never told them what we thought they should do or become, or where—or even if—they should go to college. We actively wondered along with them how God might use them for His glory, explored all the options for their lives, and did everything we could to help them achieve their goals, but we always encouraged them to make and own their own decisions. We were parenting by faith. We thank God for the choices they have made and who they have become—followers of Jesus full of His life and Spirit. We did our best to give them the life of God in our home in order to give them a life with God as adults. That should be the hope of lifegiving parenting.

For the record, here's a microprofile for Sally and me. After a quarter century of ministering to Christian parents and families through Whole Heart Ministries, we're narrowing our focus to more strategically help Christian parents raise wholehearted children for Christ. Sally will continue encouraging and ministering to Christian women and moms—online, in print, in person, and overseas. Keeping up with her grown children, and grandchildren, will be a whole new arena of ministry for her. I'll be expanding Whole Heart Press, our publishing ministry, to provide more books and resources for Christian parents, and developing our Family Faith Project to equip parents for family faith formation at home. We are both still driven by God to pursue the vision to "seek first His kingdom" with our lives. And we'll never stop being lifegiving parents.

❧   ❧

The Lifegiving Parent is a summary statement. It's truly only a fraction of what we could say—and have said over the past twenty-five years—about Christian parenting. And yet I think it is an important message we've never said this way before. Our Christian culture makes it so easy for Christian parents to get caught up in having Christian things, going to Christian places, and doing Christian activities so our children will be Christians. In other words, it's easy as a parent to mistake a Christian life for the life of Christ. It's easy to lose sight of what the real beating heart of Christianity is: the life of God. That's the unique message this book offers—that our real goal as Christian parents is not just to make sure our children become part of the Christian life but rather to make sure we as parents introduce them to the life of Christ. Our children need to see and experience the life of the living God being lived out in our homes and families.

The eight heartbeats of lifegiving parenting in this book are not intended to be a comprehensive checklist of everything you need to do. They are just ways for you to begin thinking about how to bring the life of God into your home for your children and how to make His spiritual heartbeat heard and felt by them. That's all lifegiving parenting is really about. As we started out saying in chapter 1, "Someone's Got to Give"—and that someone is you. If you know God is alive in your life, then begin to make Him alive in your home with some of the suggestions in this book. To amplify the words of Jesus, "Let your light shine before men [and your children] in such a way that they may see your good works, and glorify your Father who is in heaven" (Matthew 5:16). Remember that "your light" is His life: "In Him was life, and the life was the Light of men" (John 1:4). If you're a believer, then you should consider yourself "dead to sin, but alive to God in Christ Jesus" (Romans 6:11). That consideration is what will enable you to become a lifegiving parent, able to give your children a life worth living for Christ.

Growing Your Child's Values

WE INTRODUCED our Family Ways in chapter 7, "Shaping Your Child's Will." Below is the complete list of all twenty-four Ways. If you're interested in making the language of biblical family values part of your lifegiving parenting, you can find *Our 24 Family Ways: A Family Devotional Guide* (a workbook with 120 family devotions) and *Our 24 Family Ways: Kids Color-In Book* on Amazon.com and WholeHeart.org.

Our 24 Family Ways

CONCERNING **AUTHORITIES** IN OUR FAMILY . . .

1. We love and obey our Lord, Jesus Christ, with wholehearted devotion.

2. We read the Bible and pray to God every day with an open heart.

3. We honor and obey our parents in the Lord with a respectful attitude.

4. We listen to correction and accept discipline with a submissive spirit.

Concerning RELATIONSHIPS in our family . . .

5. We love one another, treating others with kindness, gentleness, and respect.

6. We serve one another, humbly thinking of the needs of others first.

7. We encourage one another, using only words that build up and bless others.

8. We forgive one another, covering an offense with love when wronged or hurt.

Concerning POSSESSIONS in our family . . .

9. We are thankful to God for what we have, whether it is a little or a lot.

10. We are content with what we have, not coveting what others have.

11. We are generous with what we have, sharing freely with others.

12. We take care of what we have, using it wisely and responsibly.

Concerning WORK in our family . . .

13. We are diligent to complete a task promptly and thoroughly when asked.

14. We take initiative to do all of our own work without needing to be told.

15. We work with a cooperative spirit, freely giving and receiving help.

16. We take personal responsibility to keep our home neat and clean at all times.

Concerning ATTITUDES in our family . . .

17. We choose to be joyful, even when we feel like complaining.

18. We choose to be peacemakers, even when we feel like arguing.

19. We choose to be patient, even when we feel like getting our own way.

20. We choose to be gracious, even when we don't feel like it.

Concerning CHOICES in our family . . .

21. We do what we know is right, regardless what others do or say.

22. We ask before we act when we do not know what is right to do.

23. We exercise self-control at all times and in every kind of situation.

24. We always tell the truth and do not practice deceitfulness of any kind.

Knowing Your Child's Personality

DISCOVERING AND UNDERSTANDING your child's emerging personality is like a nearsighted person getting glasses and, as my daughter Joy recently experienced, being able to see leaves on trees and bricks in walls for the first time. Life comes into focus and things begin to make sense. That's what happens when you see your child for the first time through the lens of personality.

We talked only briefly about that lens in chapter 8, "Cultivating Your Child's Character," so some additional detail will be helpful. You can find the full picture of the personality model sketched out below in my book *Educating the WholeHearted Child*. This brief introduction to that personality model will sharpen your vision enough to make "personality talk" an ongoing conversation in your family.

There are three primary elements of personality: (1) modes of thinking, (2) mental focus, and (3) life orientation. Taken together, they create a simple way of describing your or your child's personality.

Modes of Thinking
I have observed that our minds operate in two definable modes of thinking—investigation (seeking out information to gain knowledge) and determination (sorting out information to reach

conclusions). In other words, we're either looking *for* information or looking *at* information. Within each of those thinking modes, there are also two mental tasks, making four tasks in total. However, each person will tend to prefer one of the two tasks for each mode. Your personality is determined by the two mental tasks, one from each mode, that you prefer to use. Here are all the parts of that thinking picture:

THINKING MODE: INVESTIGATION

Purpose: Seeking out information to gain knowledge.

> **Mental Task: Investigating FACTS**—You seek out information based on your objective five senses. You favor the practical. You look to the proven way. You are comfortable with routine and details. You are a concreate, linear thinker.

> **Mental Task: Investigating INSIGHTS**— You seek out information based on a subjective sixth sense. You favor the possible. You look for a better way. You are comfortable with theory and the big picture. You are an abstract, global thinker.

THINKING MODE: DETERMINATION

Purpose: Sorting out information to reach conclusions.

> **Mental Task: Determining by LOGIC**—You sort out information based on impersonal logic. You are systematic, analytical, and task oriented. You strongly value competence and being correct.

Mental Task: Determining by VALUES—You sort out information based on personal values. You are relational and people oriented. You deeply value social skills and harmony in relationships.

Personality Types

There are four possible personalities that can be described from the two modes of thinking and their mental tasks. Rather than using just letters, though, we've given the personalities verb-based descriptions to make them easy to understand and remember for your children—Doer, Helper, Mover, and Shaper. Here are the four personalities:

The **DOER** Child

Two Mental Tasks: Facts + Logic

Description: "The industrious child who gets things done."

Life Motto: "I can do that!"

The **HELPER** Child

Two Mental Tasks: Facts + Values

Description: "The serving child who encourages others."

Life Motto: "How can I help you?"

The **MOVER** Child

Two Mental Tasks: Insights + Values

Description: "The inspiring child who influences others."

Life Motto: "Let's do it together."

The SHAPER *Child*

Two Mental Tasks: Insights + Logic

Description: "The imaginative child who conceives new things."

Life Motto: "I have a better idea."

Mental Focus

There is more to personality than just how you think, though. Where you focus your mental energy—externally or internally—is also important. You've heard the terms *extroversion* and *introversion*, but those words seem too cumbersome for children. We prefer the terms *active* and *reflective* to describe mental focus—active is an external focus, while reflective is an internal focus.

> **ACTIVE**—*Active children focus their mental energies and attention on the external world of people and events. These children tend to think as they speak. They are more easily distractible but typically finish tasks quickly in order to move on to something else. Their outward focus often makes them verbal and outgoing. They refuel mentally by being with other people.*

> **REFLECTIVE**—*Reflective children focus their mental energies and attention on the internal world of thoughts and ideas. These children tend to think first, then speak. They have strong powers of concentration and are slower to call a task*

finished because they can be perfectionistic. Their inward focus often makes them quiet and mysterious. They refuel mentally by being alone.

Life Orientation

Finally, there is the matter of how you prefer to orient to life—do you "do the work first" and then enjoy life, or do you "enjoy life" because the work will always get done? We've expressed the difference between these two as a preference for either time or experience. Time orientation needs predictability; experience orientation needs flexibility.

> **TIME**—*Time-oriented (TO) children value predictability, order, structure, and schedule. They are motivated to move toward decisions and seek conclusions so they can know what to expect and how to plan for it. To them, experience-oriented (EO) people can seem aimless or lazy. They get the work done first.*

> **EXPERIENCE**—*Experience-oriented (EO) children value flexibility, spontaneity, openness, and curiosity. They are motivated to keep their options open and put off decisions so they can get more input and avoid making wrong decisions. To them, TO people can seem rigid or joyless. They enjoy life first.*

Putting Personality Together

The easiest way to talk about personality is first to determine which of the four types best describes you or your child. Are you a Doer, Helper, Mover, or Shaper? That description alone will say a great deal about your general personality without any additional words. And with just four words to remember, it is the easiest way to introduce the language of personality to your child.

However, adding the mental-focus designation will draw the picture of your personality with even greater detail—so you may be an Active Doer, a Reflective Helper, an Active Mover, a Reflective Shaper, and so on. There are eight possible personality combinations, but they are easy to remember. I consider this expanded description the best way to talk about personality in your home, and one that gives enough variation to make each personality under your roof distinctive.

Finally, life orientation doesn't need to be part of your personality description, but you can also discuss whether you are time oriented (TO) or experience oriented (EO). You can talk about it as its own independent factor, or you can add it to your personality description—for example, a Time-Oriented Active Doer or an Experience-Oriented Reflective Mover. A strongly organized child might proudly defend being TO, or a strongly spontaneous child EO.

Always keep in mind, and keep reminding your children, that knowing your personality is not about comparison or being better; it's about appreciation. Personality should never be just about what makes us different but about appreciating and enjoying our differences. Observing, talking about, and celebrating how God has gifted your family with specific and different kinds of personalities will give you an appreciation for each family member and for the God who made all who live in your home.

Notes

CHAPTER 1: SOMEONE'S GOT TO GIVE

1. Vern L. Bengtson, *Families and Faith: How Religion Is Passed Down across Generations* (New York: Oxford University Press, 2013), 184–86.

CHAPTER 3: NURTURING YOUR CHILD'S SPIRIT

1. Lawrence O. Richards, *New International Encyclopedia of Bible Words* (Grand Rapids, MI: Zondervan, 1985, 1991), 591.

CHAPTER 4: GUARDING YOUR CHILD'S HEART

1. Eleanor H. Porter, *Just David* (Monument, CO: Whole Heart Ministries, 2001), 6.

2. Solomon addresses remarks both to a singular "son" and multiple "sons" in chapters 1–9, but all remarks are considered to be for all of his sons.

CHAPTER 5: RENEWING YOUR CHILD'S MIND

1. Leonard Sweet, *From Tablet to Table: Where Community Is Found and Identity Is Formed* (Colorado Springs: NavPress, 2014), 15–16.

2. Lawrence O. Richards, *New International Encyclopedia of Bible Words* (Grand Rapids, MI: Zondervan, 1985, 1991), 442.

CHAPTER 6: STRENGTHENING YOUR CHILD'S FAITH

1. See Mark 1:14-22; Luke 4:31-33; Matthew 17:1-13; 18:1-6 (NASB and NIV); 19:1-2, 13-15, 27-30; 20:20-28.

2. Lawrence O. Richards, *New International Encyclopedia of Bible Words* (Grand Rapids, MI: Zondervan, 1985, 1991), 117.

3. Ibid.

CHAPTER 7: SHAPING YOUR CHILD'S WILL

1. Clay Clarkson, *Heartfelt Discipline: Following God's Path of Life to the Heart of Your Child, 3rd ed.* (Monument, CO: Whole Heart Press, 2014).
2. Bob Dylan, "Gotta Serve Somebody," *Slow Train Coming* (New York: Columbia Records, 1979).

CHAPTER 8: CULTIVATING YOUR CHILD'S CHARACTER

1. "What Does the Bible Say about Christian Character?" GotQuestions.org, accessed November 21, 2017, https://www.gotquestions.org/Christian-character.html.
2. Isabel Briggs Myers with Peter B. Myers, *Gifts Differing: Understanding Personality Type* (Mountain View, CA: Davies-Black Publishing, 1980, 1995), 168.

CHAPTER 9: FORMING YOUR CHILD'S IMAGINATION

1. Merriam-Webster.com, s.v. "imagination," accessed November 21, 2017, https://www.merriam-webster.com/dictionary/imagination.
2. C. S. Lewis, "Bluspels and Flalansferes: A Semantic Nightmare," in *Selected Literary Essays*, ed. Walter Hooper (London: Cambridge University Press, 1969), 265, emphasis added.
3. Caryn Rivadeneira, "Theology of the Imagination," *Christianity Today*, June 18, 2014, https://www.christianitytoday.com/women/2014/june/theology-of-imagination.html.
4. Charlotte Mason, *Towards a Philosophy of Education* (Radford, VA: Wilder Publications, 1925, 2008), 40.
5. PO Bronson and Ashley Merryman, "The Creativity Crisis," *Newsweek*, July 10, 2010, http://www.newsweek.com/creativity-crisis-74665.
6. Mark Prigg, "Why Your Toddler's Vocabulary at Age TWO Can Predict Their Success in Later Life," *Daily Mail*, August 19, 2015, https://www.dailymail.co.uk/sciencetech/article-3203970/How-does-toddler-talk-Researchers-say-vocabulary-age-TWO-predict-future-success-school.html.

CHAPTER 10: ONE LIFE TO GIVE

1. For more insights on these personality comments, see "Knowing Your Child's Personality" on pages 221–26.

About the Authors

Clay Clarkson is the executive director of Whole Heart Ministries, the nonprofit Christian home and parenting ministry he and Sally founded in 1994. He has been the administrator for more than sixty ministry conferences since 1996 and is the publisher at Whole Heart Press, the publishing arm of the ministry. He has written, cowritten, and edited numerous books, and he considers himself an expository writer with a heart for communicating truth and wisdom from God's Word to strengthen Christian parents and families. Clay earned a master of divinity from Denver Seminary in 1985 and ministered on church staffs overseas and in the States before starting Whole Heart Ministries. He is also a Christian singer, songwriter, and worship leader, and he is currently developing children's illustrated storybook concepts. He and Sally have lived in fifteen homes in two countries and four states in their thirty-seven years of marriage. They now live at 7,300' in Monument, Colorado, in the shadow of Pikes Peak.

Sally Clarkson is the mother of four wholehearted grown children, a champion of biblical motherhood, and a visionary inspirer of Christian women. Her ministry reaches thousands of women every day on the SallyClarkson.com blog and AtHomeWithSally.com podcast, and by her presence on social media. She is the author or coauthor of twenty books, a popular conference speaker for more than twenty years, the heart of Mom Heart Ministry small-group outreach to mothers and Mum Heart Ministry international, and the voice of the LifeWithSally.com monthly online-streaming media subscription course for Christian women. Her recent books *The Lifegiving Home* (with Sarah Clarkson) and *The Lifegiving Table* capture her belief in and commitment to the power of home in the life of children. Sally thrives on the companionship of her family, thoughtful books, beautiful music, regular tea times, candlelit dinners at home, good British drama, walking, and traveling to see her children.

Clarkson Family Books and Resources

The Lifegiving Home: Creating a Place of Belonging and Becoming
Sally Clarkson and Sarah Clarkson (Tyndale, 2016)

The Lifegiving Home Experience: A 12-Month Guided Journey
Sally Clarkson with Joel Clarkson (Tyndale, 2016)

The Lifegiving Table: Nurturing Faith through Feasting, One Meal at a Time
Sally Clarkson (Tyndale, 2017)

The Lifegiving Table Experience: A Guided Journey of Feasting through Scripture
Sally Clarkson with Joel Clarkson and Joy Clarkson (Tyndale, 2017)

Different: The Story of an Outside-the-Box Kid and the Mom Who Loved Him
Sally Clarkson and Nathan Clarkson (Tyndale, 2017)

A Different Kind of Hero: A Guided Journey through the Bible's Misfits
Sally Clarkson and Joel Clarkson (Tyndale, 2017)

Own Your Life: Living with Deep Intention, Bold Faith, and Generous Love
Sally Clarkson (Tyndale, 2014)

Heartfelt Discipline: Following God's Path of Life to the Heart of Your Child
Clay Clarkson (Whole Heart Press, 2003, 2012, 2014—3rd ed.)

Our 24 Family Ways: A Family Devotional Guide
Clay Clarkson (Whole Heart Press, 1998, 2004, 2010, 2014)

Our 24 Family Ways: Kids Color-In Book
Clay Clarkson (Whole Heart Press, 2004, 2014)

Educating the WholeHearted Child: WholeHearted Christian Home Education for Ages 4–14
Clay Clarkson with Sally Clarkson (Apologia Press, 1996, 1998, 2011—3rd ed.)

10 Gifts of Heart: What Your Child Needs to Take to Heart before Leaving Home
Sally Clarkson (Whole Heart Press, 2013, 2017)

The Mission of Motherhood: Touching Your Child's Heart for Eternity
Sally Clarkson (WaterBrook Press, 2003)

The Ministry of Motherhood: Following Christ's Example in Reaching the Hearts of Our Children
Sally Clarkson (WaterBrook Press, 2004)

WHOLE HEART MINISTRIES™

Whole Heart Ministries is a nonprofit Christian home and parenting ministry founded by Clay and Sally Clarkson. Since 1994, our mission has been to encourage, equip, and enable Christian parents to raise wholehearted children for Christ. As a family-run ministry, our goal has been to help Christian parents through books and resources, events, and online ministries. Our current ministry initiatives include Sally Clarkson Ministry, Mom Heart Ministry, Storyformed Project, Family Faith Project, and the WholeHearted Learning Project.

For more information, visit our ministry websites or contact us.

WholeHeart.org—Information, vision, and heart of Whole Heart Ministries

SallyClarkson.com—Sally's blog, podcast, and more for Christian women

LifeWithSally.com—Monthly courses from Sally's two decades of ministry

MomHeart.com—Training and encouragement for Mom Heart small groups

Storyformed.com—Blog and resources on reading and literature for families

MyFamilyFaith.com—Blog, helps, and resources on family faith formation

Whole Heart Ministries
PO Box 3445
Monument, CO 80132

719-488-4466 | 888-488-4466
whm@wholeheart.org | admin@wholeheart.org